Juggling Your Finances:
Basic Excel Guide

SECOND EDITION

M.L. HUMPHREY

See mlhumphrey.com for titles on Microsoft Word, PowerPoint, Access and more.

CONTENTS

INTRODUCTION TO THE SECOND EDITION

I published the first edition of this book a decade ago as a companion to the book that is now titled *Budgeting for Beginners*. I honestly hadn't looked at it since, but in the meantime I have gone on to write a LOT of books about Microsoft Excel, like *Excel for Beginners*—which is a beginner title for learning Excel—as well as *Excel for Budgeting*—which walks users through how to create the budgeting worksheet I use to track my finances.

49,000 sales of Excel books later…This book has still chugged along selling a few copies here or there.

Since I'm updating the original Excel Essentials series, I figured I'd update this one as well. It was written using Excel 2007 (wow), and not many people have that anymore, so I wanted to update the screenshots this book uses to a more recent version of Excel, Excel 2024.

The basics of Excel don't change. SUM is still going to be the function you use to add numbers together. And you still refer to cells by column and row number. The appearance has definitely changed, though (and not for the better, in my opinion), so it's time to bring this book up to the present. I'd love to change the title, too, but that's just going to have to remain what it is.

The purpose of this guide is to discuss how to use Excel for basic budgeting calculations. It will walk through how to do the following calculations in Excel:

Addition:

- How much you earned in a month.
- How much you earned in a month from one specific source.
- How much you spent this month.
- The total balance in your accounts.
- The total amount you owe.

Subtraction:

- How much money will be left over after you pay your bills.

- Your net worth.

- How much of a shortfall you'll have if you're spending more than you earn.

Multiplication:

- How much you'll earn when you know the rate you'll be paid per hour or task.

- Your takehome pay from your gross pay when you know what percent you keep.

- Your takehome pay from your gross pay using a tax rate.

- Your annual expenses based on one period of expenses.

- How much you will save or be short after one year.

Division:

- How much you earn or spend on average.

- How many hours you need to work to earn a certain gross amount.

- How much you need to gross in order to take home a certain net amount.

- How many months of expenses you can cover with cash on hand.

* * *

In order to make it as easy as possible to learn the basics of using Excel for addition, subtraction, multiplication, and division, the main chapters of this book focus only on how to do those mathematical computations. However, if you work in Excel to any great extent, you will quickly find that you need to perform a number of other tasks, such as widening columns, bolding text, and formatting numbers.

The Tips and Tricks chapter at the end covers those topics, and when I use one of those tricks I'll let you know. You'll likely refer to it often as you work through this guide.

As a side note, it's a really, really good idea to be comfortable enough with math that you can judge whether an answer makes any sense or not. Excel is a tool, and the calculations in a worksheet are only as good as the person creating and using them. If you put in the wrong information, or set up a formula wrong, you will get a wrong answer. You need to be able to gut check your results.

Okay then, let's get started with some basic definitions.

BASIC EXCEL DEFINITIONS

Before we start, I want to make sure we're using the same words to describe things.

If you're familiar with Excel this may seem very basic, but it's a good idea to skim through anyway, just to be sure. All the screenshots in this book are from Excel 2024, but the definitions and descriptions should apply to any version of Excel from Excel 2007 onward.

Column

Excel uses columns and rows to display information. Columns run across the top of the worksheet and, unless you've done something funky with your settings, are identified using letters of the alphabet.

As you can see below, they start with A on the far left side and march right on through the alphabet (A, B, C, D, E, etc.). If you scroll far enough to the right, you'll see that they continue on to a double alphabet (AA, AB, AC, etc.) and, in some versions of Excel, a triple alphabet (AAA, AAB, AAC, etc.)

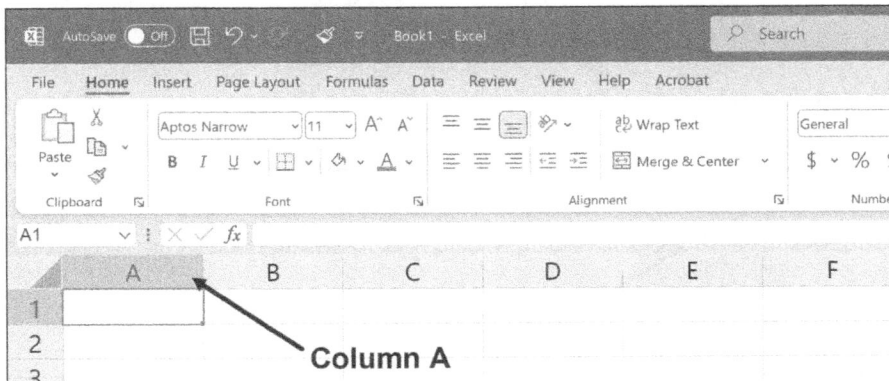

Column A

Row

Rows run down the side of the worksheet and are numbered starting at 1 and up to a very high number that will not matter for what you're doing here.

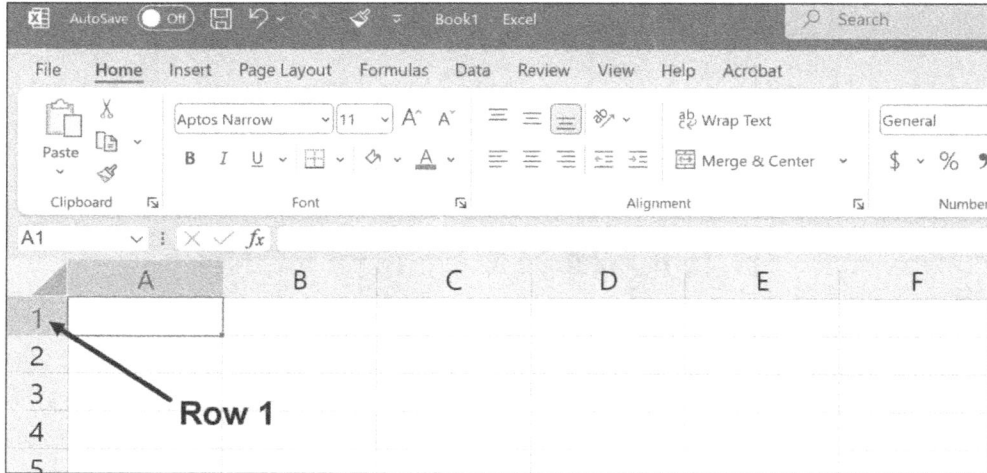

Cell

A cell is a combination of a column and row that is identified by the letter of the column it's in and the number of the row it's in. When you've clicked on a specific cell it will have a darker border around the edges, like you can see for Cell A1 below.

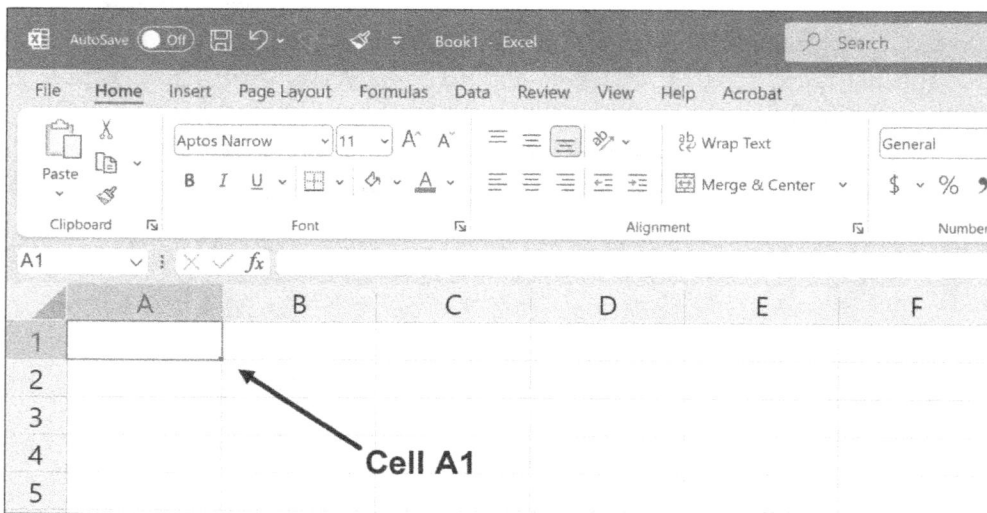

Click

If I tell you to click on something that means to use your mouse (or trackpad) to move the cursor on the screen over to a specific location and left-click or right-click on that location. (See the next definition for the difference between left-click and right-click).

If you left-click, this generally selects the item. If you right-click, this generally creates a dropdown list of options to choose from. If I don't tell you which to do, left- or right-click, then left-click.

Left-Click/Right-Click

If you look at your mouse or your trackpad, you generally have two flat buttons to press. One is on the left side, one is on the right. If I say left-click, that means to press down on the button on the left. If I say right-click, that means press down on the button on the right.

(If you're used to using Word or Excel you may already do this without even thinking about it. Also, some newer trackpads don't make it as obvious where to left- or right-click so you may need to experiment a bit.)

Cursor

If you didn't know this one already, your cursor is what moves around when you move the mouse (or use the trackpad). In Excel it often looks like a three-dimensional squat cross or it will look like one of a couple of varieties of arrow. The different shapes you see mean that different functions are available at that time. If something isn't working for you, try moving your mouse around just a bit until the cursor changes its appearance, and then try again.

Spreadsheet

I'll try to avoid using this term, because it can mean your worksheet or your workbook. Apologies if I fail at that.

Worksheet

A worksheet is a combination of rows and columns that you can enter data in. When you open a new Excel file, it opens to Sheet1. The name is visible at the bottom left of your workbook.

Some versions of Excel had multiple worksheets available when you opened a new workbook, newer versions only have one available.

If you ever need more worksheets, you can add them. There should be some form of a + sign down at the bottom of the workbook that will let you do this:

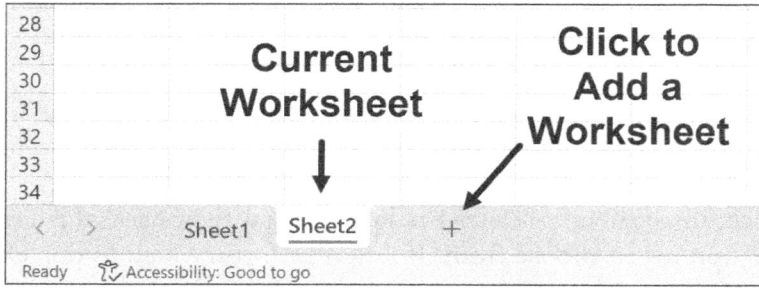

The worksheet with its name highlighted in white and underlined is the one you're currently viewing. To move between worksheets, just click on the name of the one you want.

Formula Bar

The formula bar is the long white bar at the top of the screen with the $f\chi$ symbol next to it. If you click in a cell and start typing, you'll see that what you type appears not only in that cell, but in the formula bar.

When you enter a formula into a cell and then hit Enter, the value returned by the formula will be what displays in the cell, but the formula will still appear in the formula bar when you click back on that cell.

Tab

I refer to the various choices at the top of the screen as tabs. In Excel 2024 the options are File, Home, Insert, Page Layout, Formulas, Date, Review, View, and Help. (I also have an Acrobat one, but I don't think that's standard for all users. Prior versions of Excel didn't have File and Help available up there, so this can fluctuate a bit.)

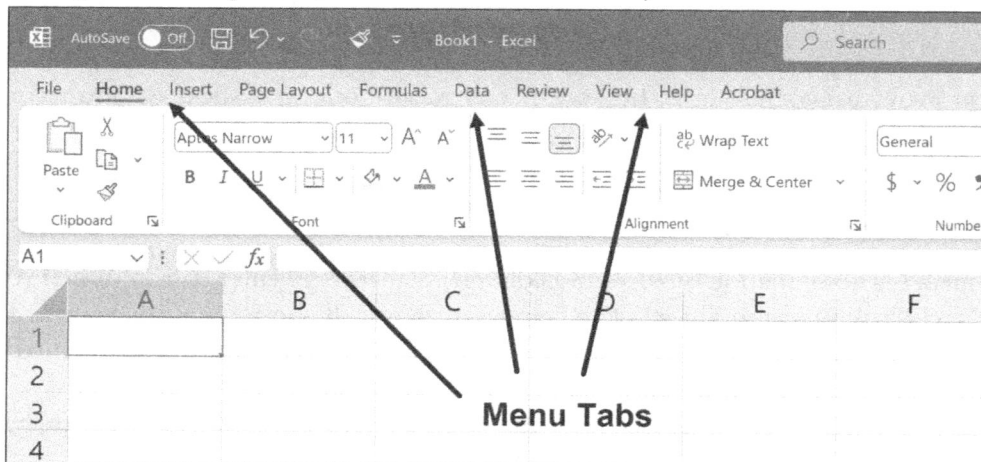

Each menu tab you select will show you different options.

On the Home tab above you can see options for copy/cut/paste, format cells, edit cells, and insert/delete cells, for example. The Home tab is the main tab you'll use for what we're going to discuss in this book.

Scrollbar

Scrollbars appear when there is more information than you can see on the screen. I don't expect to need them in this book, but here's an example of one in the font dropdown menu which has a scrollbar because there are more fonts than can be displayed on the screen at one time:

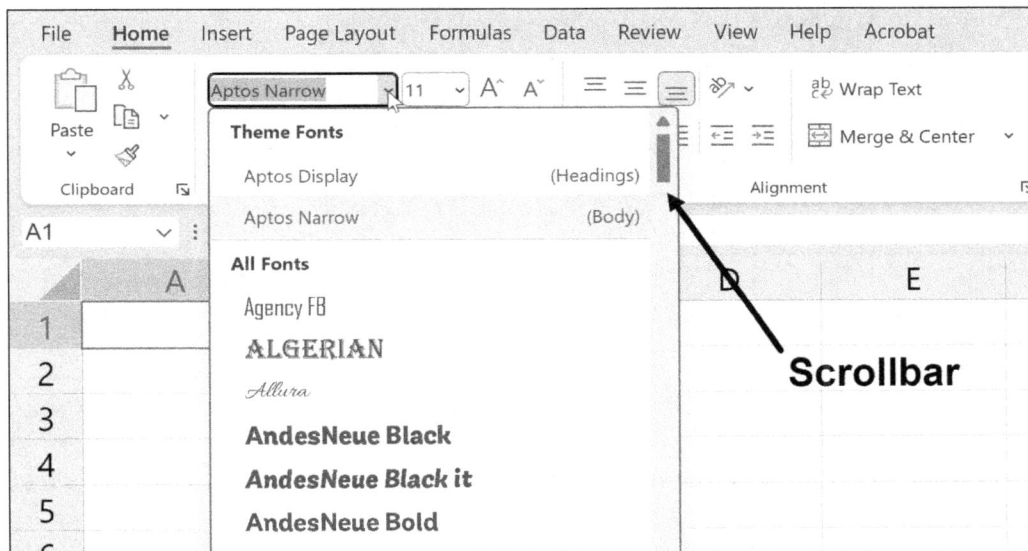

Scrollbars appear on the right-hand side or bottom of a list or worksheet when needed.

You will see a dark bar in a light gray area. You can then left-click on that bar, hold the left-click, and drag to move through the list or worksheet.

You can also left-click in the light gray area to either side of the bar, or left-click on the arrows at the ends of the scrollbar space. Each will move you through the list or worksheet, just at different increments.

Data

I use data and information interchangeably. Whatever information you put into a worksheet is your data.

Select

If I tell you to "select" cells, that means to click on them so they're highlighted.

If the cells are next to each other, you can just left-click on the first one you want, and drag the cursor (move your mouse or finger on the trackpad) until all of the cells are highlighted.

When you select a group of cells that are located next to one another like this, they'll all be surrounded by a darker border, and all of the cells will be shaded except for the first one you clicked on. Like so:

Selected Cells

Here I clicked and dragged from Cell A1 to Cell D7. You can see that Cell A1 is white, but the rest of the cells are shaded gray.

If you want to select cells that are not next to each other or that don't form a rectangle when selected, then you need to use the Ctrl key.

Select the first cell or range of cells you want, hold down the Ctrl key (bottom left of my keyboard), and select the next cell or range of cells you want.

Keep using Ctrl to select more cells until done.

Each cell or group of cells you've previously selected will be shaded in gray. The last cell or group of cells will be shaded like above where the first cell in that selected range is white with a border.

The border will be lighter than when one single cell is selected.

Here I selected Cells A1 through B2, A5 through A7, C4 through D5, and then I selected Cell C7:

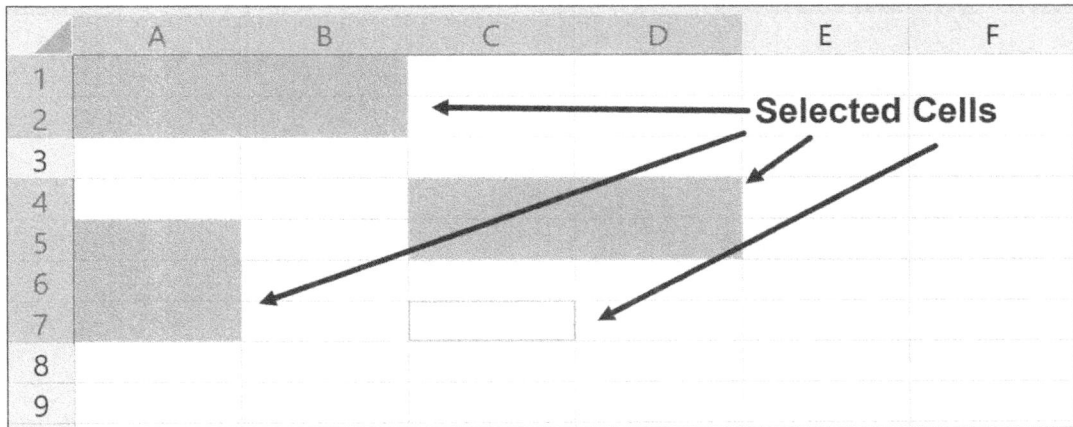

Arrow

If I say that you can "arrow back" to something that just means to use the arrow keys to navigate from one cell to another.

For example, if you enter information in Cell A1 and hit Enter, that moves your cursor down to Cell A2. If you now want to go back to Cell A1, you can just arrow back to it using the up arrow.

(You can also just left-click in Cell A1. It does the same thing. But sometimes using the arrow keys is quicker than having to switch over to your mouse or trackpad. It's always useful to learn how to perform common tasks with the keyboard when you can.)

Formula

A formula is a calculation that you have Excel perform. It can be basic math or it can use functions.

Function

A function is a short-hand way to tell Excel to perform a series of steps. So, SUM, for example, tells Excel to add the values that you provide.

I will write functions in all caps, like I did above with SUM, but you can type them into Excel without using all caps.

ADDITION: OVERVIEW

There are at least four different ways to perform addition in Excel, some more useful than others. In this chapter I'll walk you through each of them, and then in the next chapter we'll apply them to real-world examples. My best practice when working with formulas is to make the values I'm working with visible, so in the next chapter I'm not going to use this first one, but it's good to know how to do anyway.

Option 1: Put The Entire Formula In A Cell

Your first option is to simply type the entire formula into a cell using the plus (+) sign to indicate addition. When you hit Enter Excel will display the result.

So, for example, if I wanted to add 15, 45, and 35, I would click into a cell and type the following, and then hit Enter:

$$=15+45+35$$

Excel will then display the result of that calculation (95) in that cell.

Note the use of an equals sign at the start there. That is how you tell Excel that you want it to perform a calculation. You can also use a minus (-) or plus (+) sign to start a formula, but I don't recommend it. Excel will just convert it over to an equals sign anyway, and it's easier to remember that starting with an equals sign means you're writing a formula.

If you arrow back to a cell that used a formula, you'll be able to see the formula (=15+45+35) in the formula bar:

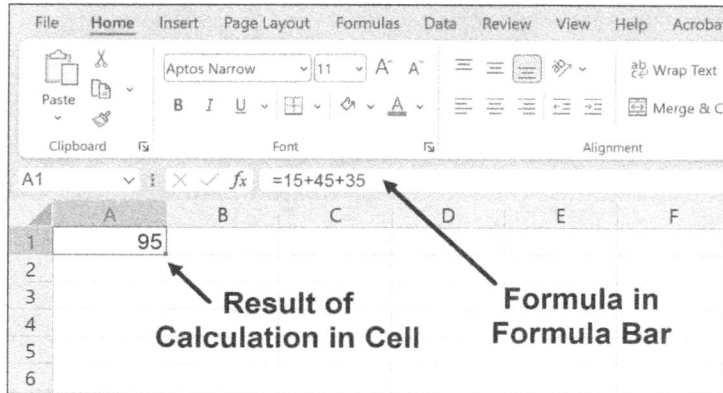

You can also double-click on a cell to see the formula in that cell. Just be careful with that. Because sometimes when you double-click on a cell, Excel thinks you want to edit the contents of that cell, and if you then click on another cell, Excel will try to add that cell reference into your existing formula.

If that ever happens to you, the easiest thing to do is just use Esc to back out of what you were doing. (Esc is on the top left corner of my keyboard.)

Your other option is to hit Enter, and then use Ctrl + Z (hold down the Ctrl key and the Z key at the same time) to undo the last thing you did.

Option 2: Put Your Values in Cells in Excel and Then Select the Cells With the Values You Want to Add

Your second option is to put the values you want to add together into cells in your worksheet, and then select them.

For example, if I put the number 15 in Cell A1, the number 45 in Cell A2, and the number 35 in Cell A3, I can then select all three of those cells to see what they add up to.

(To do that, either left-click and drag from Cell A1 or Cell A3 to select all three cells, or use Ctrl to select each one separately.)

Excel will display the sum of the numeric values in a range of selected cells in the bottom right corner of the worksheet (below the scroll bar).

Note that this only works if Excel views those numbers as numbers. If you entered them yourself, that shouldn't be an issue. But sometimes for copied data or data you received from someone else, Excel views numbers as text instead, and then you'll only see a count value in that bottom corner.

By default, for numbers Excel will display the Average, Count, and Sum of the values in your selected cells. In this case, the average is 31.66666667, the count is 3, and the sum is 95:

Average: 31.66666667   Count: 3   Sum: 95

If you don't see Sum as one of your options, then right-click in the space that shows those values. You will see a dropdown menu that has a lot of choices. Towards the bottom of that menu will be a list of what calculations can potentially display in this space.

In addition to Average, Sum, and Count, you can also have Numerical Count, Minimum, and Maximum.

Each one that has a check next to it will display a result as appropriate. (Only Count displays for text entries.)

Left-click on each one to add or remove a check so it will or won't display:

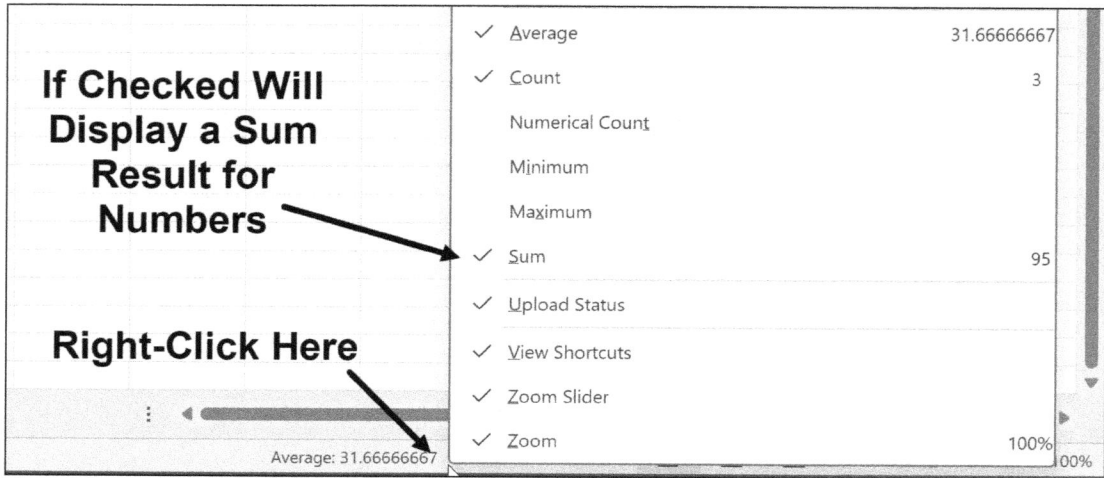

Note that you have to select more than one cell to see a result in that section.

Option 3: Enter Your Own Formula

Sometimes the easiest option is to just write your own formula.

To add things together in Excel, the basic function to use is SUM, and the basic formula is:

$$=SUM(\ )$$

where what you put in the parens is what gets added together.

Within the parens, you can use a comma to separate entries. It's the equivalent of saying "and". So,

$$=SUM(2,3)$$

would give a result of 5 because it's telling Excel to sum the value 2 *and* the value 3.

$$=SUM(2,3,4)$$

would give a result of 9 because that is summing 2 *and* 3 *and* 4.

Although, honestly, if you're going to directly enter numbers like that, you can go back to Option 1 and just use

$$=2+3+4$$

instead.

The real power of the SUM function comes when you reference to a range of cells and use the colon (:) separator, which is the equivalent of telling Excel "through". For example, if I write A1:A5, that means Cell A1 through Cell A5.

In other words, Cells A1, A2, A3, A4, and A5.

Put that with SUM and we get:

$$=SUM(A1:A5)$$

to add together the values in those five cells, which is much easier than writing out the entire list.

Using a colon tells Excel to include all of the cells that form a rectangle between the first listed cell and the last one. Here, for example, you can see which cells Excel would add together for the formula =SUM(A1:D9):

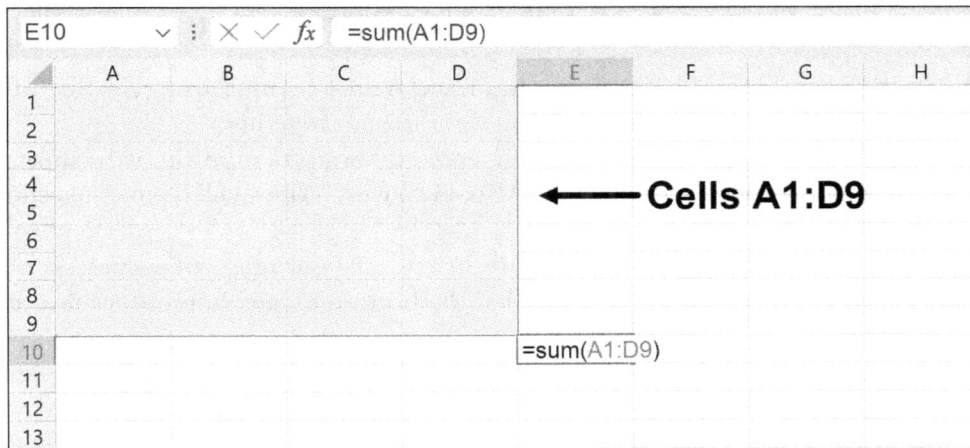

So going back to our simple example from Option 2 where we put our values in Cells A1, A2, and A3, we could write:

$$=SUM(A1:A3)$$

and get the exact same result of 95.

Now, you may be thinking that it sounds hard to have to remember how to write the correct cell range in a formula. Good news is that Excel is designed to help with that.

You can start typing your formula, and then select the cells you want to include with your mouse or trackpad, and Excel will write the cell reference portion of the formula for you.

Try it. Go to any cell, and type

$$=SUM($$

and then select the cells you want to add together (left-click and drag for cells next to each other or left-click and use Ctrl for cells that aren't next to each other).

Once you've chosen all the cells you want, type in the closing paren, and hit Enter.

You should see the value of all of the cells you selected added together in the cell. Click back on that cell to see the formula in the formula bar that Excel used.

If you're not sure you chose the right cells, double left-click in the cell with your formula. Excel will highlight all of the cells that were used like in the image above where it selected Cells A1 through D9.

If the formula you ended up with uses more than one cell reference, each group of cells referenced in the formula will be outlined with a different color, and the corresponding reference in the formula will be color-coded to match.

(Remember if you start accidentally messing up your formula after you do this that Esc is the way to back out of what you're doing.)

Option 4: Use the AutoSum Button

Another option is AutoSum. What it does is has Excel write a formula using the SUM function for you by guessing the range of cells that you want to sum together.

It requires you to have your values already entered somewhere in the worksheet, and to either have them in a single row or column. Also, ideally the values will be in consecutive cells with no breaks between values.

Once you've done that, click into the cell at the end of your range of values, so either the cell to the right of a row of values or the cell at the bottom of a column of values, and then click on AutoSum.

In my version of Excel AutoSum is in the Editing section of the Home tab in the top right corner. It looks like a pointy uppercase E (the sum function from math):

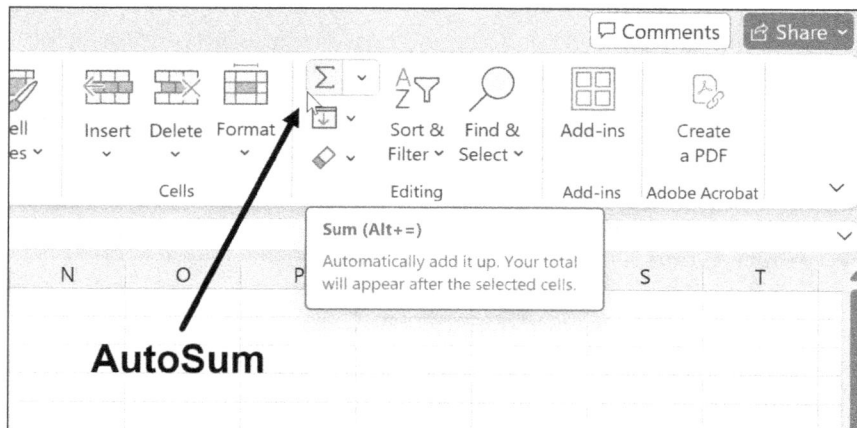

AutoSum

(In older versions of Excel it also had the word AutoSum next to it. They removed that because in newer versions of Excel you can do more than just add values together by using the dropdown arrow to choose a different function.)

Here I've used AutoSum for values that were in Cells A1 through A3. I clicked into Cell A4 and then clicked on the AutoSum option.

The formula Excel suggested is:

$$=SUM(A1:A3)$$

Perfect. I can now hit Enter and I'll see the result of that formula, 95, in Cell A4.

If I then click back onto Cell A4, I'll see the formula it suggested in the formula bar.

The key to using AutoSum is making sure that Excel actually selects all of the cells that you want it to. If there's a gap in your numbers, so a blank column or row, Excel will generally only select the cells prior to the gap.

So, if you had values in Cells A1through A3 above, then A4 and A5 were blank, and then there were more values in A6 and A7, AutoSum would only capture A6 and A7.

(This is where being able to at least guesstimate what a value should be will help you tremendously. It lets you do a reality check on the numbers you're seeing. Remember, a worksheet is only as accurate as the person who creates it and the person who uses it. It's also why it's good to know the basics of writing your own formulas, including how to read cell notation)

In Excel 2024 at least, you don't have to be in the cell directly next to the list of values for AutoSum to work. As long as there is nothing in the cells in between, it should still write a SUM formula for you from the top value to the cell directly before that one. But I'm almost certain that was not the case in the past, so be careful and always check the formula Excel suggests before you accept it.

ADDITION: EXAMPLES

Now let's walk through some real-life examples. (And yes, here in the year 2025 these are probably laughable, but we want easy to enter numbers, so don't worry if they aren't realistic.)

Example 1: How much did you earn this month?

Let's say you:

- Housesit three times last month and were paid $25, $40, and $35.

- You also earned $52.23 from your retail job.

- And you were paid $10, $8, and $12 for dogwalking.

Step 1: Input the Information Into Excel

First step is to put all this information into a worksheet in Excel. Personally, I tend to include more information than I think I'll need, because I find it easier to input it all up front than have to go back later and add it in when I decide I need it.

So, open Excel and input the information into the first available worksheet:

	A	B	C	D	E
1	Source	Income Type	Date Paid	Amount Paid	
2	Jones Family	Housesitting	1/1/2025	$25.00	
3	Smith Family	Housesitting	1/16/2025	$40.00	
4	Lopez Family	Housesitting	1/10/2025	$35.00	
5	Snack Shack	Day Job	1/28/2025	$52.23	
6	Dogwalk Lucy	Dogwalking	1/15/2025	$10.00	
7	Dogwalk Lucky	Dogwalking	1/22/2025	$8.00	
8	Dogwalk Pepper	Dogwalking	1/31/2025	$12.00	

Above is what my worksheet looks like after I've entered the information above.

As you can see, I used Row 1 to name my columns. In this case I have four columns called Source, Income Type, Date Paid, and Amount Paid. I did this by clicking in each cell and typing in the text I wanted to see.

I recommend always using the top row to name your columns and trying to limit your headers to just that one row. I am a big fan of using the filter function in Excel, but it doesn't work well if you use more than one row for your column headers.

(Of course, the filter function works better the more recent the Excel version you're working in. Another reason to consider upgrading if you're using an older version of Excel.)

What I did above looks simple, but there are a number of tricks I used to make it look like it does.

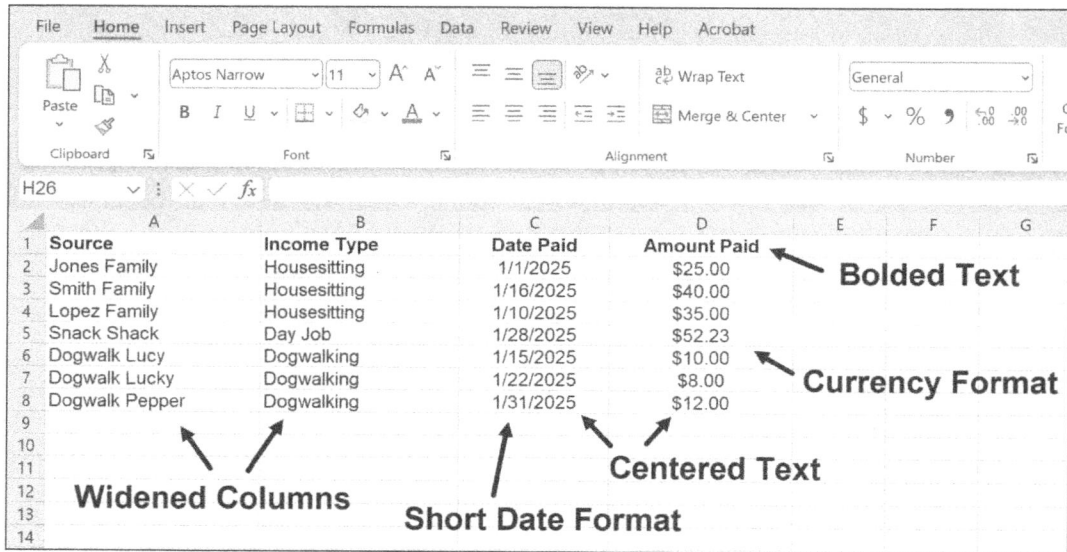

I don't want to distract from the basic math functions we're trying to learn here, so each of these is discussed in detail in the tips and tricks section at the end of the book under the headings: Date Formatting, Currency Formatting, Bold Text, and Column Width.

As a matter of fact, if this is the first time you've worked in Excel, I'd recommend reading through that section once now just to get familiar with what you can do in Excel besides the basic math functions we're discussing here. (Or, go read *Excel for Beginners* first, which assumes you know nothing about Excel and walks you through 95 percent of what you need to know to use it day-to-day.)

Step 2: Add Up Your Numbers

Okay. Back to the example.

We entered our information into Excel. Now we need to determine our earnings. There are three options we can use.

Option 1: Select the cells in the Amount Paid column, and look at the value in the bottom right corner under Sum.

◢	A	B	C	D	E
1	**Source**	**Income Type**	**Date Paid**	**Amount Paid**	
2	Jones Family	Housesitting	1/1/2025	$25.00	
3	Smith Family	Housesitting	1/16/2025	$40.00	
4	Lopez Family	Housesitting	1/10/2025	$35.00	
5	Snack Shack	Day Job	1/28/2025	$52.23	← **Select**
6	Dogwalk Lucy	Dogwalking	1/15/2025	$10.00	**Cells**
7	Dogwalk Lucky	Dogwalking	1/22/2025	$8.00	
8	Dogwalk Pepper	Dogwalking	1/31/2025	$12.00	
9					

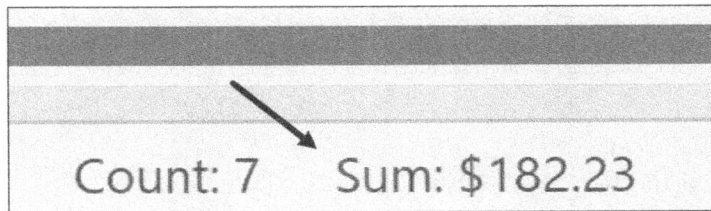

Count: 7   Sum: $182.23

Option 2: Type a formula into any cell that doesn't already contain information using SUM to add the values for Amount Paid.

In this case I would use:

=SUM(D2:D8)

or

=SUM(D:D)

That first formula references the specific cells that have values in them (D2:D8), but sometimes I prefer to use the second formula example instead. It references all of the cells in Column D (D:D), so that if I add more information into the worksheet my total will update to include that information automatically.

The only trick to referencing the entire column is that your formula has to be in a different column so you don't get a circular reference and you can't have any other values in that column.

Also, note that I'm not listing putting a formula with actual values in a cell as an option. That's because if you use specific values in your formula and then later change one of those values, your formula will be wrong and it won't be easy to see.

Of course, you will need to update the values in the cells if they change, but it's much easier to see when that needs to happen.

Putting the values in their own cells also lets you use those values for multiple calculations without having to enter them each time.

Option 3. Use AutoSum.

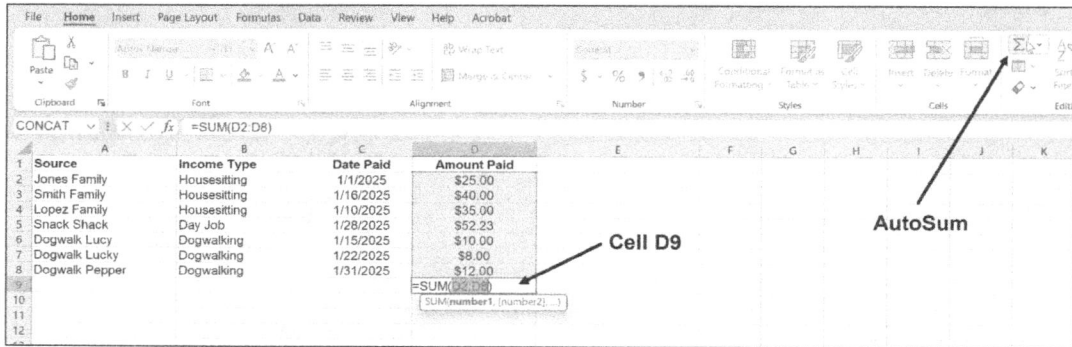

Above I clicked into Cell D9 and then clicked on AutoSum.

Excel suggested a formula of=SUM(D2:D8). Once I was sure that's the formula I wanted (mostly by looking at the selected cells), I hit Enter.

* * *

You should get $182.23 as your answer.

* * *

Example 1B: How much did you earn from *housesitting* this month?

Option 1. Select the three cells that relate to amount paid for housesitting and look at the value in the bottom right corner.

This is the best approach for when you just want a quick answer and won't need to see the result each time you open the worksheet. It should be $100.

Option 2. Type a SUM formula into any cell that doesn't already contain information, including only the values related to housesitting:

If your data isn't going to change or update, you could manually figure out which cells contain data related to housesitting. In this case they're all together so I can use:

=SUM(D2:D4)

But in a situation like this it's better to use SUMIF. What SUMIF does is it takes a range of values like we have in this table and lets you sum only those values that meet your criteria. In this case, those where the income type was housesitting.

=SUMIF(B2:B8,"Housesitting",D2:D8)

If I put housesitting into Cell C12, I can use a cell reference instead for the criteria input:

=SUMIF(B2:B8,C12,D2:D8)

or

=SUMIF(B:B,C12,D:D)

All three of those are saying, "When the value in Column B is "housesitting" then include the value in Column D in the SUM calculation."

Note that it is not case-sensitive, so will match both Housesitting and housesitting.

* * *

Note that I couldn't use AutoSum for this scenario since I had multiple sources of income for the period.

* * *

Example 2: How much did you spend this month?

Let's assume you had the following expenses for the month:

- Rent of $500
- Car insurance of $125
- Utilities of $75
- Credit card of $425

Step 1: Input the Information Into Excel

I did this in a new worksheet that I called Expenses. See the definition of worksheet for how to add a new worksheet if you're working in a version of Excel that only starts you off with one.

My data looks like this:

	A	B	C
1	**Expense**	**Amount**	**Date Due**
2	Rent	$500.00	1/1/2025
3	Car Insurance	$125.00	1/15/2025
4	Utilities	$75.00	1/23/2025
5	Credit Card	$425.00	1/16/2025
6			
7			

I bolded the text, widened columns, formatted dates, formatted currency, centered text, and renamed the worksheet.

Step 2: Add It Up

I would use one of three options to add the values.

Option 1: Highlight the cells in Column B and look in the bottom right corner for the value.

If you have a lot of values in a column and no other values there, you can select the entire column by clicking on the letter for that column. So in this case, the B. All cells in that column should then show as selected, and the total under Sum that you'll see in the bottom right corner will include all cells in Column B that have a numeric value in them.

Option 2: Enter a formula in any blank cell in the worksheet that adds the four values in the Amount column.

In this case:

=SUM(B2:B5)

If I used a cell that wasn't in Column B, I could also use:

=SUM(B:B)

Option 3: Use AutoSum.

I could click into Cell B6 (or since this is Excel 2024, Cell B7 or B8 or B9, etc.) and then click on AutoSum and let Excel write the formula for me. Once I was satisfied that it covered the values I wanted, I'd hit Enter.

If the formula isn't what you want, just click into the formula bar and change it.

* * *

You should get $1,125 as your answer.

* * *

Example 3: What is the total balance available in your accounts?

Let's assume you have:

- $1,542.21 in one checking account

- $3,500 in a savings account, and

- $921.42 in a second checking account.

How do you find the total value in all three accounts?

Step 1: Input the Information Into Excel

I did this in a new worksheet that I called Assets.

It looks like this:

	A	B	C	D	E
1	**Account**	**Balance**			
2	Checking A	$1,542.21			
3	Savings A	$3,500.00			
4	Checking B	$921.42			
5					
6		**$5,963.63**	=SUM(B2:B5)		
7					

Same formatting used as before. Also you can see the result of adding the cells up in Cell B6 and the text of the formula I used in Cell C6.

Step 2: Add It Up

You have three choices for adding the amounts:

1. Select the cells in Column B and look in the bottom right corner for the value.

2. Enter a formula anywhere in the worksheet that adds those three cells. In this case:

$$=SUM(B2:B5)$$

Note that because I put the SUM formula into Cell B6, I decided to include Cell B5 in my formula. Because it's currently blank it doesn't change the result, but it does make sure that if I add more information into this listing in Row 5, my formula will capture it. It should also update the formula if I choose to insert rows.

3. Use AutoSum in Cell B5, B6, etc.

* * *

You should get $5,963.63 for your total balance.

* * *

Example 4: What is the total amount you owe?

This is always a painful one to calculate, especially if you've just been blindly paying minimum payments and not looking at the total balance owed.

Let's assume you have:

- One student loan in the amount of $8,432.21,

- Another in the amount of $4,563.78,

- A credit card in the amount of $473.99, and

- Another credit card in the amount of $3,789.21.

Step 1: Input the Information Into Excel

I did this in a new worksheet that I called Liabilities. It looks like this:

	A	B	C	D	E
1	**Account**	**Balance**			
2	Student Loan A	$8,432.21			
3	Student Loan B	$4,563.78			
4	Credit Card A	$473.99			
5	Credit Card B	$3,789.21			
6				**$17,259.19**	=SUM(B2:B5)
7					

Note here that I put the SUM formula into Cell D6 but that the range of cells I'm summing up is still in Column B. It isn't where you put the formula that matters, it's where the information you want to analyze is located.

Also, in the original of this book this screenshot had a typo. I had called both student loans "Student Loan A". If you make an error like that, a quick way to fix it is to click on the cell with the error and use F2. That will take you to the end of the text in the cell. You can then backspace to delete the A and replace it with a B.

Step 2: Add It Up

Here I would also use one of three choices to add up the values:

1. Select the cells in Column B and look in the bottom right corner for the value.

2. Enter a formula anywhere in the worksheet that adds those four cells:

=SUM(B2:B5)

or

=SUM(B:B)

I could only use the second option if the formula wasn't in Column B.

3. Use AutoSum in Cell B6, B7, etc.

* * *

Whichever way you choose, you should get $17,259.19 for your total amount owed.

SUBTRACTION: OVERVIEW

There isn't an equivalent to the SUM function for subtraction. You just have to write the calculation out.

The basic Excel formula for subtracting things is:

$$=()-()-()$$

The first number you put in parens is your starting number. Any numbers after that are the numbers you're subtracting from the first number.

Option 1: Put The Entire Formula In A Cell

I don't recommend it, but one option for subtraction is to type the entire calculation in a cell.

So, for example, if I wanted to subtract 35 from 45, I could click into a cell and type the following:

$$=45-35$$

If you do that, when you hit Enter the cell should show you the value 10. If you then arrow back up to the cell you just used, you'll see the formula (=45-35) in the formula bar above the worksheet.

Option 2: Use Cell References

Option 2 is to put the values you want to use into other cells and then reference them with a formula.

$$=A1-B1$$

There is a trick to make this easier when you have a lot of values you need to subtract. That is to combine the subtraction sign with the SUM function. Like this:

$$=(\ )-SUM(\ )$$

Where the first entry is what you're subtracting from, and the cell range in the SUM function is all the values you want to subtract from it.

Let me show you an example:

	A	B	C	D	E	F	G	H
1	45	10	15	20				
2						**Result**	**Formula**	
3						0	=A1-B1-C1-D1	
4						0	=A1-SUM(B1:D1)	
5								
6								
7								
8								

In Row 1 we have the value 45 in Cell A1, and then the values 10, 15, and 20 in Cells B1 through D1.

If I want to subtract the values in Cells B1 through D1 from the value in Cell A1, I can write that out:

$$=A1-B1-C1-D1$$

But I will get the same result if I use:

$$=A1-SUM(B1:D1)$$

The nice thing is that you can expand this trick to include as many values as you need to. When it's just three values you want to subtract, there's not much difference. But try manually writing a subtraction formula for 1,000 values. Oof. No.

So those are your two options for subtraction. Type a formula directly into one cell (not recommended) or create your own formula, ideally leveraging the use of the SUM function.

Pretty simple, really.

SUBTRACTION: EXAMPLES

Now let's walk through some examples using the types of calculations you'll want to perform to get a handle on your finances.

Example 1: How much money will be left after you pay your bills?

Let's use the numbers above and say that you have $5,963.63 in your accounts.

We already calculated that your expenses for the month were $1,125.

After you pay those bills, how much will you have left?

You could write:

$$=5963.63-1125$$

and you'd get $4,838.63.

But that's prone to error. Better to use a formula that references the cells that already have those values in them.

Fortunately, you can add or subtract values that are on different worksheets. (You can even do this across Excel files, but we're not going to go there right now.)

In this example, the $5,963.63 value is on our Assets worksheet and the $1,125 is on our Expenses worksheet.

We can pull those numbers together in one of two ways.

Option 1: Pull the value from the Expenses worksheet into the Assets worksheet and then subtract.

	A	B	C	D	E
1	**Account**	**Balance**			
2	Checking A	$1,542.21			
3	Savings A	$3,500.00	**Formulas Used**		
4	Checking B	$921.42			
5					
6	Total Assets	$5,963.63	=SUM(B2:B5)		
7				**Reference**	
8	Monthly Expenses	$1,125.00	=Expenses!B9	**to Cell on**	
9				**Different**	
10	Amount Leftover	$4,838.63	=B6-B8	**Worksheet**	
11					
12			**Results**		
13					

Column C shows the three formulas used in this worksheet. (If you have Excel 2024 or later there is a function called FORMULATEXT that lets you show the formula being used in a cell by referencing that cell with the function. Otherwise to do this just copy the text of a formula to a new cell and then put a single quote at the start of the text.)

The first formula, used in Cell B6, is a simple SUM formula. The second, in Cell B8, pulls in the value from the other worksheet:

=Expenses!B9

Rather than try to write that myself, I typed:

=

and then navigated to the Expenses worksheet by clicking on the worksheet tab name. There I clicked on the cell that contained my expenses per month amount, which in this case was Cell B9. And then I hit Enter.

Now Cell B8 in the Assets worksheet has the same value as Cell B9 in the Expenses worksheet.

(Your cell references may be different depending on where you chose to put your formulas. So just focus on the idea that you can start a formula and click on the cell in any worksheet that you want to use and Excel will write that reference for you.)

After I did that, it was just a matter of simple subtraction in Cell B10. In this case:

=B6-B8

Option 2: Pull the information into a new worksheet.

To return just the result, in a new worksheet type = into a cell, click on the Assets worksheet, click on the cell with the value you want, type the minus sign (-), click on the Expenses worksheet, click on the cell with the value you want there, and then hit Enter.

You could also pull in each value separately and then use basic subtraction to calculate the result of assets minus expenses.

Here's what the two options look like in the same worksheet:

	A	B	C	D	E
1	Option 1		Result	Formula	
2			$4,838.63	=Assets!B6-Expenses!B9	
3					
4	Option 2		Result	Formula	
5	Total Assets		$5,963.63	=Assets!B6	
6	Total Expenses		$1,125.00	=Expenses!B9	
7	Left at End of Month		$4,838.63	=C5-C6	
8					
9					
10					

Column C is where the formulas actually are. Column D is showing the text of each of the formulas.

Under Option 1, the entire calculation is made in one cell:

$$=Assets!B6-Expenses!B9$$

That's saying take the value from Cell B6 on the Assets worksheet and subtract from it the value from Cell B9 on the Expenses worksheet.

Note how when Excel references a cell in a different worksheet than the one you're in, it lists the worksheet name (Expenses or Assets here) followed by an exclamation sign (!) before the cell number from that other worksheet.

When Excel references cells in the current worksheet, you just see the cell reference like so:

$$=C5-C6$$

Under Option 2, the values were brought over from the other worksheets into Cells C5 (=Assets!B6) and C6 (=Expenses!B9), and then the calculation was made in Cell C7 using a minus sign and references to those cells (=C5-C6).

Example 2: Your Net Worth

You can calculate your basic net worth by taking all of your assets minus all of your liabilities. It's basically a calculation of what you'd have left if you took everything you have and paid off everything you owe.

We won't get into it here (I do in *Budgeting for Beginners* and in *Excel for Budgeting*), but I find basic net worth a fairly worthless number. Liquid net worth (what you could actually get after fees and penalties are paid) is far more valuable in my opinion.

But we'll calculate basic net worth anyway.

Same process as above, except this time we take the total of all of the assets and subtract all of the liabilities.

You can do it in the Assets worksheet, the Liabilities worksheet, or in a new one.

Here I did the calculation for the total assets and liabilities within the formula itself, and in a new worksheet:

	A	B	C	D	E
E20			fx		
1	Net Worth	$ (11,295.56)	=SUM(Assets!B2:B4)-SUM(Liabilities!B2:B5)		
2					
3	**Result** ↗		↖ **Formula Used**		
4					

If you see numbers in parens in a field, like how I have $(11,295.56) in Cell B1 here, that means the number is a negative number.

Which is not ideal for net worth but not all that uncommon for many people, especially those just getting started. (The key to keeping your head above water is to focus on something I call short-term liquid net worth, which is basically having enough money to pay your bills for the next month or two even if it means you have longer-term debt.)

Okay then.

The formula I used here is:

=SUM(Assets!B2:B4)-SUM(Liabilities!B2:B5)

I built this by typing

=SUM(

in Cell B1, navigating to the Assets worksheet, selecting Cells B2 through B4, typing

)-SUM(

navigating to the Liabilities tab, selecting Cells B2 through B5, and then typing

)

and hitting Enter.

Sounds like a lot, but it's mostly just clicking around to find the cells you want to use.

If that's confusing, then create a summary value on both the Assets and Liabilities tabs first. Then your formula can just reference the cell that contains those totals. Like so:

=Assets!B6-Liabilities!D6

where Cell D6 on the Liabilities worksheet contains the total of all the liabilities and Cell B6 on the Assets worksheet contains the total of all the assets.

Example 3: The Amount of Your Shortfall

You might've noticed that with the numbers we're using here, you are earning less than your monthly bills

In our example, you earned $182.23 in January but spent $1,125, which means a shortfall of $942.77.

Fortunately, you had money in the bank to pay your bills, so you were actually able to pay them, but if you hadn't, that would've been how much more you needed to earn to pay everyone you owed.

To calculate the shortfall in Excel, find where you want to make the calculation, type in =, go to the Income worksheet, click on the cell with the total income for the month, type in the – sign, go to the Expenses worksheet, click on the cell with your total expenses for the period, and hit Enter.

You should get $(942.77) or -942.77 depending on how you have the cell formatted. The formula will look something like this:

='Income (2)'!D9-Expenses!B9

where Cells D9 and B9 are the respective cells in each of the worksheets that have the total income and expenses for the period, and Income (2) and Expenses are the names of the respective worksheets that contain the information.

Note here that because there are spaces in the name of the income worksheet, Excel puts a single quote at the start and end of the name.

'Income (2)'

One final point. The order of the entries matters for subtraction. If I had put

=Expenses!B9-'Income (2)'!D9

instead, my result would be a positive $942.77, which would be wrong. With addition, it doesn't matter. With subtraction, it absolutely does.

So be sure your numbers make sense when you're done.

* * *

One final comment. It should be obvious, but I'll say it anyway: Any formula in Excel can reference cells in different worksheets not just ones that use subtraction.

Okay, then, on to multiplication.

MULTIPLICATION: OVERVIEW

There are two main ways to multiply values in Excel.

Option 1: Put The Entire Formula In A Cell

For multiplication you use the asterisk (*) sign to indicate multiplication.

So, for example, if I wanted to multiply three times five, I would write:

$$=3*5$$

in a cell. When I hit Enter, the cell will show the value 15.

Option 2: Use Cell References

The basic Excel formula for multiplying things is:

$$=()*()*()$$

where the cell references in each set of parens contain the values to use for the multiplication.

There is also a function you can use for multiplication, PRODUCT, but I rarely use it.

$$=PRODUCT()$$

Usually I'm only multiplying two numbers together and using the asterisk is faster, but PRODUCT works better with cell ranges.

For example, here is a situation where I'm multiplying price per unit times number of units times a percent that provides 10% off the total:

	A	B	C	D	E	F	G
1	**Price Per Unit**	**# Bought**	**After Discount**				
2	$2.50	2	90%				
3					$4.50 =A2*B2*C2		
4					$4.50 =PRODUCT(A2:C2)		
5							
6							
7							
8							

I can either use

$$=A2*B2*C2$$

or

$$=PRODUCT(A2:C2)$$

Using PRODUCT here is less prone to error and takes only one input instead of three. Note that with multiplication, the order of the inputs doesn't matter.

$$=C2*A2*B2$$

would generate the same result.

MULTIPLICATION: EXAMPLES

Now let's walk through some real-world examples that require multiplication.

Example 1: How Much You'll Earn Given a Known Pay Rate

Multiplication basically makes adding the same number over and over again easy. Which comes in handy if you have, for example, a job that pays an hourly wage.

Let's say you're trying to figure out the gross (so this is before taxes or anything else) amount that you'll earn at your new retail job.

When they hired you, they told you your hourly pay was going to be $8.25.

How much can you expect to earn next month if you work twenty hours a week and there are four weeks in the month?

To figure that out you'd multiply the amount you earn per hour ($8.25) times the number of hours you're going to work (20) times the number of weeks you'll work (4).

If you just input the formula it will look like this:

$$=8.25*20*4$$

The answer you get is 660.

Better, though, to put those values in cells instead. That way you can see what went into the calculation:

▲	A	B	C	D	E	F	G
1	Wage	Hrs/Week	Weeks		Gross Pay	Formula Used	
2	$8.25	20	4		$660.00	=A2*B2*C2	
3					$660.00	=PRODUCT(A2:C2)	
4							
5							
6							
7							

Here I can use either

$$=A2*B2*C2$$

or

$$=PRODUCT(A2:C2)$$

* * *

I want to pause here and once again make an argument for learning enough math to understand when an answer doesn't make sense. You're never going to double-check your work unless you know what you're doing well enough to understand that something isn't right.

Excel is a great tool, but it's only as good as the person using it.

I also want to repeat that checking your cell references in your formula is one key troubleshooting step. To do so, double-click on the cell with your formula in it.

Excel will color each individual cell or cell range reference in the formula a different color. It will also outline the cell(s) that match each reference in that color.

Here, for example, I double-clicked on Cell E2, which contains my formula, and Excel colored A2 in the formula blue, B2 red, and C2 purple. It also outlined each of those cells in their matching color. So Cell A2 is blue, for example, to match the blue of A2 in the formula text. I can then see if everything is as expected. Are the cells with the values I expect to be multiplied actually outlined in a color? Are they outlined in a separate color each? And so on.

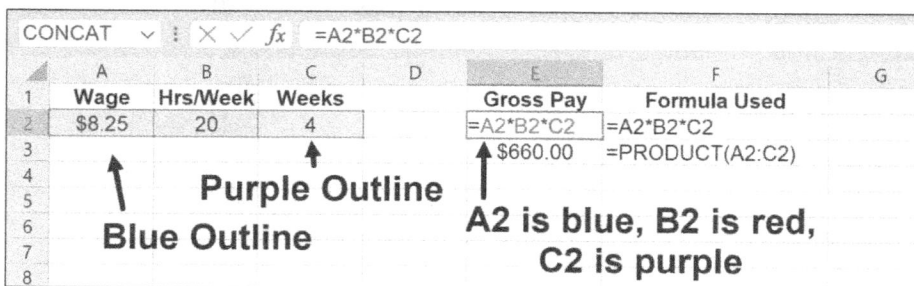

CONCAT	⌄ ⋮ × ✓ *fx*	=A2*B2*C2					
▲	A	B	C	D	E	F	G
1	Wage	Hrs/Week	Weeks		Gross Pay	Formula Used	
2	$8.25	20	4		=A2*B2*C2	=A2*B2*C2	
3					$660.00	=PRODUCT(A2:C2)	
4							
5		**Purple Outline**					
6					**A2 is blue, B2 is red,**		
7	**Blue Outline**				**C2 is purple**		
8							

You can also see the color-coding for formula components if you click into the formula bar when clicked onto a cell with a formula in it.

Example 2: Calculating Your Net Earnings When Your Takehome Percent Is Known

Unless you're doing cash-based work (like housesitting), or you have an exemption from taxes—like certain individuals with very low incomes—or you're self-employed and expected to pay taxes yourself, chances are when you get paid it won't be the gross amount (hours times pay rate). It will instead be that amount minus some percent for taxes, retirement, etc.

How much that percent is will be specific to you.

For simplicity's sake, let's assume that you make the same amount every pay period. Further, let's assume that you know what your take-home pay is on average compared to your gross income, and that you've figured out that for every dollar you earn, you only get 82 cents in your paycheck.

That means that your take-home pay (or net pay) is 82% of your gross pay.

You can now use that information and multiplication to figure out how much you'd take home at various hours per week worked.

	A	B	C	D	E	F
1	Wage	Weeks				
2	$8.25	4				
3						
4						
5			Hrs Per Week	Gross Pay	% Takehome After Tax	Takehome Pay
6			20	$660.00	82%	$541.20
7			30	$990.00	82%	$811.80
8			40	$1,320.00	82%	$1,082.40
9			50	$1,650.00	82%	$1,353.00
10			60	$1,980.00	82%	$1,623.60
11						
12						
13	Formulas In Row 6			=$A$2*$B$2*C6		=D6*E6
14	Formulas In Row 10			=$A$2*$B$2*C10		=D10*E10
15						

In Cell A2 we have an hourly wage of $8.25 and in Cell B2 we have an assumption of four weeks of work. In Column C I've listed various hours per week from 20 up to 60.

Column D uses multiplication to calculate gross pay based on those values.

We already saw this calculation in Example 1, but the location of each value is different.

I typed a formula into Cell D6 that uses 20 hours per week, from Cell C6:

$$=A2*B2*C6$$

That's great, but I don't want to have to rewrite it for each row. I want to copy this down to the other rows in Column D. Excel will adjust the reference to Cell C6 for me just fine. But the problem is that Excel also wants to adjust the references to Cells A2 and B2 for me, and I don't want it to do that. To prevent Excel from changing those references, I need to use dollar signs in front of the column and row values to fix the cell reference.

I changed the formula to:

$$=\$A\$2*\$B\$2*C6$$

That let me then copy that formula to Cells D7 through D10 and get the result I expected. The formula in Cell D10 is now:

$$=\$A\$2*\$B\$2*C10$$

My reference to Cells A2 and B2 remained fixed, but the reference to Cell C6 adjusted. Perfect.

In Column E I've listed the percent of pay that's actually taken home: 82%. (On average, that could change drastically if the numbers are too far off your baseline that gave you that percentage.)

To get the takehome pay in Column F, we can then just multiply gross pay by the percent in Column E.

The formula in Cell F6 is:

$$=D6*E6$$

When I copied it down to Cell F10 it becomes:

$$=D10*E10$$

Great. Done.

Example 3: Calculating Net Earnings Using a Known Tax Rate

What if want to use a tax rate instead? In this case, 18%?

Then you'd need to combine subtraction and multiplication in the equation.

If you know that your tax rate is 18%, you also know that what you take home from your gross pay is 100% minus 18%.

Here I copied the data from before over to a new set of columns, and changed the third column to show the tax rate of 18%.

I then had to also change the takehome pay calculation in the fourth column of data.

The equation for what is now Column N becomes:

$$=L6*(1-M6)$$

That's gross pay times 100% minus the tax rate.

	I	J	K	L	M	N	O
1	Wage	Weeks					
2	$8.25	4					
3							
4							
5			Hrs Per Week	Gross Pay	Tax Rate	Takehome Pay	
6			20	$660.00	18%	$541.20	
7			30	$990.00	18%	$811.80	
8			40	$1,320.00	18%	$1,082.40	
9			50	$1,650.00	18%	$1,353.00	
10			60	$1,980.00	18%	$1,623.60	
11							
12							
13	Formulas In Row 6			=$A$2*$B$2*K6		=L6*(1-M6)	
14	Formulas In Row 10			=$A$2*$B$2*K10		=L10*(1-M10)	
15							

You need the parens there to make sure that you are multiplying the tax rate by the right amount. Otherwise, Excel would multiply the gross pay (L6) by 1 and then subtract the tax rate (M6). The parens tell it to do the subtraction first before any multiplication.

The order in which Excel performs calculations works the same as what you learned in school about what order to do calculations in. Left to right. In parens first. Etc.

And remember, if that's too complex, you can always break out each step separately. Like this:

	P	Q	R	S	T	U	V	W
1	Wage	Weeks						
2	$8.25	4						
3								
4								
5			Hrs Per Week	Gross Pay	Tax Rate	Taxes Paid	Takehome Pay	
6			20	$660.00	18%	$118.80	$541.20	
7			30	$990.00	18%	$178.20	$811.80	
8			40	$1,320.00	18%	$237.60	$1,082.40	
9			50	$1,650.00	18%	$297.00	$1,353.00	
10			60	$1,980.00	18%	$356.40	$1,623.60	
11								
12								
13	Formulas In Row 6			=$A$2*$B$2*R6		=S6*T6	=S6-U6	
14	Formulas In Row 10			=$A$2*$B$2*R10		=S10*T10	=S10-U10	
15								

Here I copied over my table, and added a column to calculate taxes paid (gross pay times tax rate). The final calculation for takehome pay then became gross pay minus taxes.

Same answer each time, regardless of how we approach it.

Example 4: Your Annual Expenses Based Upon
One Period of Expenses

Another way to use multiplication in managing your finances, is to project how much money you'll need for an entire year based upon how much you spend in a particular period, such as a month.

We already calculated that you would need $1,125 to pay your monthly expenses.

If you know that your monthly expenses will be the same for the entire year, how much money do you need to cover all of your expenses for the year?

Well, there are twelve months in a year, so you need twelve times $1,125.

I went back to the Expenses worksheet and added that formula in Cell B11. The result is $13,500.

	A	B	C	D
1	Expense	Amount	Date Due	
2	Rent	$500.00	1/1/2025	
3	Car Insurance	$125.00	1/15/2025	
4	Utilities	$75.00	1/23/2025	
5	Credit Card	$425.00	1/16/2025	
6				
7				
8				
9	Monthly Expenses	$1,125.00	=SUM(B2:B5)	
10				
11	Annualized Amount	$13,500.00	=B9*12	
12				

The formula I used was:

$$=B9*12$$

* * *

Keep in mind, that if you're annualizing your expenses that's the amount you need to actually get paid. In other words, you need to take home at least $13,500.

So if you were offered a job that paid a salary of $13,500, it wouldn't be enough to cover your bills. You'd need to earn enough to not only pay your bills, but cover the amounts that are taken out of each paycheck.

Also, remember that we all have unexpected expenses come up. So either add an amount on top of your regular expenses or include that in your estimate for each month. (And again, I go into detail about these concepts in *Budgeting for Beginners*. This book was originally written to help people who read that book use Excel to do the calculations discussed there.)

Example 5: How Much You Will Save or Be Short After One Year

You can also use the numbers we've discussed to calculate your savings or shortfall for a year.

	P	Q	R	V	W	X	Y
1	Wage	Weeks			Annual Expenses	$13,500.00	
2	$8.25	4					
3							
4							
5			Hrs Per Week	Takehome Pay	Annualized	Save/Lose	
6			20	$541.20	$7,035.60	-$6,464.40	
7			30	$811.80	$10,553.40	-$2,946.60	
8			40	$1,082.40	$14,071.20	$571.20	
9			50	$1,353.00	$17,589.00	$4,089.00	
10			60	$1,623.60	$21,106.80	$7,606.80	
11							
12							
13	Formulas In Row 6			=S6-U6	=V6*13	=W6-$X$1	
14	Formulas In Row 10			=S10-U10	=V10*13	=W10-$X$1	
15							

I put in X1 the annualized expense amount. This is the goal for takehome pay.

In Column W I multiplied takehome pay for four weeks by 13 to get the amount that would be earned in a year, since there are 52 weeks a year.

For example, the value in Cell W6 is from:

$$=V6*13$$

Once both are annualized, we can then just use subtraction to figure out the amount saved or amount short for the year. For Row 6 that formula is:

$$=W6-\$X\$1$$

Note the use of the $ signs for X1 so that the formula can be copied to the rest of the rows.

What this tells us is that if you worked 20 hours a week, you'd fall short by almost $6,500, but if you worked 40 hours a week, you'd be a little bit ahead. About $571.20, for the year. Of course, this is all based on this set of numbers. Your numbers will not be the same.

DIVISION: OVERVIEW

Just like with subtraction, there are really only two ways to divide values in Excel.

Option 1: Put The Entire Formula In A Cell

First, you can just enter the formula into any cell and hit Enter. In Excel you use the forward slash (/) to indicate division.

The basic Excel formula for dividing things is:

$$=(\ )/(\ )$$

As with subtraction, the order of the inputs matters with division, so be sure to put the number you want divided first and the number you want to divide by second.

So, for example, if I wanted to divide 15 by 5, I could start typing in the cell I'm already in or left-click on a different cell and enter the following:

$$=15/5$$

When you hit Enter, the cell should show you the value 3. If you then arrow back up to the cell you just used, you'll see the formula, $=15/5$, in the formula bar above the worksheet and the value, 3, in the cell.

Option 2: Use Cell References

The other option is to put the values in other cells in your worksheet and then write a formula that references those values. For example,

$$=A1/B1$$

would divide the value in Cell A1 by the value in Cell B1. Like here:

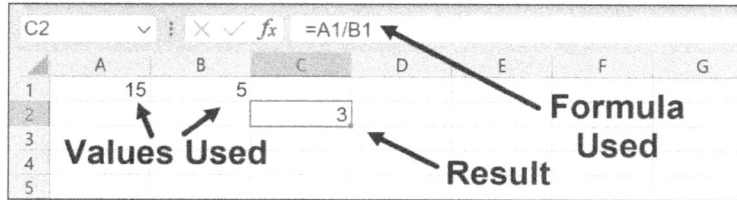

To create this, I just clicked in Cell C2, typed =, clicked on Cell A1, typed /, clicked on Cell B1, and hit Enter.

You can see that I then arrowed back to Cell C2 to see the formula in the formula bar:

For division, there are no fancy shortcuts that I know of. You just have to manually enter or click on each cell you want to include.

Although, for those of you eager to do something more complicated, you can use division in complex formulas that perform other calculations as well, like addition or subtraction, on either side of the division.

For example, I could write a formula that adds the values in Cells A1 and B1 together and then divides the total by Cell C1:

$$=(A1+B1)/C1$$

Note the use of parens around A1 and B1 to make sure that Excel adds the values in Cells A1 and B1 first before dividing the total by the value in Cell C1.

If I didn't use the parens and instead wrote this:

$$=A1+B1/C1$$

Excel would divide the value in Cell B1 by the value in Cell C1 first, and then add that result to the value in Cell A1.

* * *

We touched on it before, but let's touch on it again. Excel follows a specific set of rules for the order in which it will perform mathematical calculations. Remember those math lessons from school about what to do first? It's that.

This is called the math order of operations.

Basically, Excel calculates starting on the left side of the equation and moves to the right.

Multiplication and division have precedence over addition and subtraction. So, Excel will go through an equation and do all multiplication and division starting on the left side and moving to the right. Then it'll go back to the start and do all addition and subtraction next. Again moving from left to right.

But anything you put in parens gets calculated first. Although, within the parens, that order is followed again.

If you're going to write complex formulas that include more than one calculation, you need to be very comfortable with how this works.

To research it further, look up Operator Precedence in Excel's help or on their website.

For me, when writing a new complex formula, I will sometimes calculate each step separately so I can compare the result from doing it that way to my formula result. They need to match or I have a misplaced paren somewhere.

Once again, I will encourage you to get comfortable enough with math to be able to tell if something isn't working the way it should be.

You don't need to know how to multiply 2,531 times 3.94 in your head, but you should at least know that 2,500 times 4 is 10,000 and that your answer when you do multiply 2,531 times 3.94 should be around that and not 10.

* * *

Okay, enough of that little digression. If you didn't follow it, don't worry. Not everyone will want to use complex formulas in their spreadsheets and you can manage your finances just fine without them.

I just wanted to throw that in there for the few readers who are chomping at the bit to do something a little more complicated.

Now on to some examples of how to apply division to your finances.

DIVISION: EXAMPLES

Example 1: How Much You Earn or Spend on Average

Let's say you're trying to put together a budget, but there are certain things you do that aren't consistent. Maybe you housesit sometimes, but not on a regular schedule.

Should you just forget that income altogether? No.

What about using the most you earn each month? Also, no.

What about the least? Better, but still probably not.

If you consistently earn money from housesitting but not the same amount each month, the best bet is to probably use division to calculate an average. The more variation in the numbers month-to-month, the trickier doing this becomes.

Not from a math perspective. Math doesn't care. From a budgeting perspective. If the numbers range from $10 to $1000 and your average is $500, but it's rare to earn that much in any given month, you don't want to use that.

But right now we're just talking about basic math and how to use it, so let's walk through an example where it would be fine to use.

Say you've been housesitting for six months now and you've earned the following amounts each month: $110, $200, $45, $80, $50, and $175.

How much did you earn total for those six months?

$$=110+200+45+80+50+175$$

$660.

How much did you earn on average?

To get an average you take the total amount for the period, and divide it by the number of observations in the sample. In this case, $660 was earned over the course of six months.

The average is $110.

If you wanted to type that all into one cell it would look like this:

$$=(110+200+45+80+50+175)/6$$

But that doesn't leverage what Excel can do for you. So let's walk through your other options for calculating an average. I'm going to put months in Column A and then values in Column B with my SUM formula for the six months in Cell B9.

Option 1: Select the Cells And Look In the Bottom Right Corner of the Worksheet

Just like with Sum, Average is one of the values that Excel will display for you by default in the bottom right corner for a selected range of cells (B2:B7 here) that have numeric values in them.

Just be sure that you input a zero if you want to include an observation that doesn't have a value. So a month where you didn't make money, for example.

If you leave a cell blank, it won't include that cell in the count of the number of observations. Which is nice, when you select a range of twelve cells but only have six months of information so far. Excel will just average those six months that you actually know something about.

But it can be a problem if you have months where you earned nothing.

Option 2: Write the Formula Yourself

I already showed you above how to do that in one cell, although I do not recommend that approach. Another option is to use cell references.

	A	B	C	D	E	F
1	**Month**	**Income**				
2	January	$110				
3	February	$200				
4	March	$45				
5	April	$80				
6	May	$50				
7	June	$175				
8				**Average**	**Formula Used**	
9	**Total**	$660		$110	=B9/6	
10				$110	=SUM(B2:B7)/COUNT(B2:B7)	
11				$110	=AVERAGE(B2:B7)	
12						
13						

Here, since I already put the sum of the values in Cell B9 and we know we have six months of results, I could just write in Cell D9:

$$=B9/6$$

Option 3: Use the SUM and/or COUNT Functions with Division

Of course, I didn't need to sum the values in Cell B9 first. I could have just written:

$$=SUM(B2:B7)/6$$

That uses the SUM function to sum up my values and then I manually told Excel how many months to use for the average.

Better yet. I can get Excel to tell me how many months by using the COUNT function, which looks for how many cells in the range have a numeric value in them:

$$=SUM(B2:B7)/COUNT(B2:B7)$$

That is really the best option so far. It doesn't rely on any sort of manual input or calculation. But there's an even easier option.

Option 4: Use the AVERAGE Function

Excel actually has a function, AVERAGE, that is meant to take the average of a range of values. The basic formula is:

$$=AVERAGE\ (\ )$$

where you include in the parens the values you want to average.

In this case, the specific formula is then:

$$=AVERAGE(B2:B7)$$

The nice thing with both SUM/COUNT and AVERAGE is that I could set it up for the entire year right now, and as I add values for the rest of the year it will adjust the calculation. I've done that here in Columns A through E:

	A	B	C	D	E	F	G	H	I	J	K	L
1	Month	Income					Month	Income				
2	January	$110					January	$110				
3	February	$200					February	$200				
4	March	$45					March	$45				
5	April	$80					April	$80				
6	May	$50					May	$50				
7	June	$175					June	$175				
8	July			Average	Formula Used		July	$0		Average	Formula Used	Fixed
9	August			$110	=B15/6		August	$0		$55	=H15/12	Number of
10	September			$110	=SUM(B2:B13)/COUNT(B2:B13)		September	$0		$55	=SUM(H2:H13)/COUNT(H2:H13)	Months
11	October			$110	=AVERAGE(B2:B13)		October	$0		$55	=AVERAGE(H2:H13)	
12	November						November	$0				
13	December						December	$0				
14					Leave Blank to							
15	Total	$660			Not Include		Total	$660			Put Zeros to Include in	
16					These Months						COUNT and AVERAGE	
17											functions	
18												

Columns G through K show what happens if you only have results for half the year but are taking an average using all twelve months. Because I put zero values in there in Column H,

COUNT and AVERAGE treat this as a twelve-month period. And obviously that gives a much different result than summing those values and dividing by just six.

Bottom line: Only use manual calculations like =B15/6 or =H15/12 when you have set data that will not adjust over time. If the data will adjust, use AVERAGE or SUM/COUNT and include the full range of cells that will ultimately have values in them. Leave fields blank if you don't want to include them. Put a zero if you do.

* * *

Also, as mentioned before, if you ever want to display the contents of a cell as text, you can put a single quote at the start of the text, and Excel will treat the contents of that cell as text no matter what comes next. (Very useful for entries like January 2020 that you don't want Excel to convert to dates.)

Example 2: How Many Hours You Need to Work to Earn a Certain Gross Amount

You can also use division to figure out how many hours you need to work per month to cover your expenses.

Let's assume your shortfall for the month is $942.77, and that you are paid $8.25 an hour at your job.

But that's not what you take home, right? You only take home 82% of that. So how many hours do you need to work in a month more than you already are to cover that shortfall based on what you actually take home?

Here we go:

	A	B	C	D	E
1		Value	Formula		
2	Hourly Rate	$8.25	#N/A		
3	Tax %	18%	#N/A		
4	Takehome %	82%	=1-B3		
5	Actual Takehome	$6.77	=B2*B4		
6					
7	Need to Earn	$942.77	#N/A		
8					
9	Hrs Needed	139	=B7/B5		
10	Hrs Needed/Wk	35	=B9/4		
11					
12	Combined Calculation	35	=(B7/B5)/4		
13					
14					

Cell B2 has your hourly rate. Cell B3 has the tax rate. In Cell B4 we calculated the percent you keep based on that tax rate. In Cell B5 that gives an actual takehome of $6.77 using

$$=B2*B4$$

(You can see the text of all of the formulas in Column B in Column C. Note that any value in Column C that has an #N/A means there was no formula used, it's just a constant value that I typed in.)

Now that we have the actual amount you take home, we can calculate the number of hours you need to work in a month to cover your shortfall.

Cell B7 has the amount of the shortfall. We can then divide that by the takehome amount from Cell B5:

$$=B7/B5$$

We see that result, 139, in Cell B9. You can take that a step further and divide by 4 to get the number of hours per week that are needed. I did that in Cell B10:

$$=B9/4$$

If you want to be fancy, you can actually combine those last two calculations into one. You will see that I use parens to force Excel to perform the calculation in the right order even when they aren't needed. It's a best practice that forces me to think through the correct order of the calculation I want:

$$=(B7/B5)/4$$

That was one way to approach the problem. You could also take 942.77, divide it by 8.25 first, and then divide that by .82, and then that by 4.

Example 3: How Much You Need to Gross In Order to Take Home a Certain Amount

Another way to approach this problem is to figure out how much you need to gross in order to make enough to meet your shortfall.

So, how do you calculate the actual amount you need to earn in order to be able to take home $942.77?

By using division and the estimated percent of your pay that you take home.

If $942.77 is what you need to take home, there's a number out there (the gross pay) that when it's multiplied by the percent of your pay that you actually receive (82% in our example from above) will give you $942.77.

That's A x B = C where C is 942.77 and B is 82%.

Solve the equation above for B and you get B=C/A, which means if you divide C (942.77) by A (82% or .82) you'll know how much you need to earn.

Here's what that approach looks like.

	A	B	C	D	E	F	G
1		Value	Formula			Value	Formula
2	Takehome %	82%			Tax Rate %	18%	
3	Need to Take Home	$942.77			Need to Take Home	$942.77	
4							
5	Need to Make	$1,149.72	=B3/B2		Need to Make	$1,149.72	=F3/(1-F2)
6							

Cell B2 has the takehome percent, Cell B3 has what you need to take home to cover your expenses, and Cell B5 has what that means you need to earn, which is $1,149.72.

As discussed above, the formula for Cell B5 is:

$$=B3/B2$$

(A quick reminder here, that what I'm doing when I show you the formulas is just showing you what's happening in that other cell where you see the result. You are not going to see the formulas in your worksheet next to your results.)

I put a different approach to this question in Columns E through G in the screenshot above. There I used the tax rate of 18%, which meant the formula I wrote had to use 1 minus that tax rate. And that you can see is:

$$=F3/(1-F2)$$

where tax rate is in Cell F2, and takehome amount needed is in Cell F3.

Example 4: How Many Months of Expenses You Can Cover with the Current Amount of Cash in the Bank

This one is pretty simple compared to the others, but very handy to know if you're spending more than you're earning, which can happen. For example, you may become unemployed and need to know how many months you have before you need new income.

Or maybe you're starting up a business and living on savings. It happens.

I also use this as a "how soon will I be in trouble" measure.

So how do you do it?

Take the amount you have in the bank, and divide by how much you spend each month.

I'm going to do this on the Assets tab where I have the amount in the bank already (in Cell B6) as well as the amount of monthly expenses (in Cell B8) from our earlier example where we calculated an amount leftover:

	A	B	C	D
1	Account	Balance		
2	Checking A	$1,542.21		
3	Savings A	$3,500.00		
4	Checking B	$921.42		
5				
6	Total Assets	$5,963.63	=SUM(B2:B5)	
7				
8	Monthly Expenses	$1,125.00	=Expenses!B9	
9				
12	Number of Months Covered	5.3	=B6/B8	
13				

Based on that, the formula I need is:

$$=B6/B8$$

The answer here is 5.3 A handy number to know. (And ideally you want to keep this at 3 or above. But many people don't manage that. If nothing else, try to keep this number greater than 1 so you know you have this month's expenses covered no matter what happens. I personally do that even if it means carrying a little more debt than I'd like. Because being able to paying this months' bills without bouncing checks is more important than being debt-free.)

If I hadn't already had those numbers totaled up and in that worksheet, I could've also used:

$$=SUM(Assets!B2:B4)/SUM(Expenses!B2:B5)$$

which takes the sum of the values in the Assets worksheet in Cells B2 through B4 and divides that by the sum of the values in the Expenses worksheet in Cells B2 through B5.

Note where the parens are for each SUM function versus the slash for the division.

CONCLUSION

Alright. That's it. That's basic math using Excel and budget concepts to teach you.

The next chapter gives you a brief overview of some of the other Excel functionality I used here to format the data we were working with.

If you want to build an Excel worksheet that you can use on an ongoing basis to monitor your finances, I wrote a book that walks through how to set up the Excel workbook I use to track my assets, liabilities, income, and expenses called *Excel for Budgeting*.

(You can also just buy the workbook itself on my Payhip store if you don't want to build it from scratch, but it does have a lot of moving parts and I do think creating it from scratch helps you learn the various components it uses.)

If you want to learn more about Excel, I do have multiple series of books about Excel in general. *Excel for Beginners* is the starting point. There are versions of that book for Excel 2019, Excel 365/Excel 2021, and Excel 2024 as well as the more generic one that is meant to work with any version of Excel.

If you made it through this book, though, you may not need it. Although it does also cover topics like sorting and filtering data.

Those series continue with an *Intermediate Excel* title which covers pivot tables, conditional formatting, charts and more.

And then each series also has at least one book that goes in depth on Excel formulas and covers at least fifty functions, including functions related to text, dates, and more.

But you don't need to keep buying books from me if you're happy to look things up yourself. Excel has tremendous help options available.

These days I go to their website, since I have all of the annoying bells and whistles they keep adding turned off, which disables the Help available within Excel.

I just do a web search for something like "microsoft excel sum function", ignore the AI result at the top, and find the support.microsoft.com result:

> **Microsoft Support**
> https://support.microsoft.com › en-us › office › sum-fu ...
>
> ## SUM function
>
> The **SUM function adds values**. You can add individual values, cell references or ranges or a mix of all three. For example: =SUM(A2:A10) Adds the values in ...
>
> **Microsoft Support**
> https://support.microsoft.com › en-us › office › use-the...
>
> ## Use the SUM function to sum numbers in a range
>
> Use the SUM function to sum numbers in a range · **Type =SUM in a cell, followed by an opening parenthesis** (. · To enter the first formula range, which is called an ...

Easy enough.

Okay, then.

Let's cover those tips and tricks I used here to make things pretty, and then you're done.

EXCEL FORMATTING AND NAVIGATION TIPS AND TRICKS

I tried to keep the earlier sections of this guide limited to how to perform basic mathematical functions in Excel, but if you're going to spend any amount of time working in Excel, then you need to learn how to format cells and navigate your way around.

That's what this section is for. It's an alphabetical listing of different things you might want to do.

Add a New Worksheet

When you open a new Excel file, you'll have at least one worksheet available and maybe as many as three, depending on your version of Excel.

If you need more than that, click on the plus sign located to the right of your current worksheet(s). Here is what it looks like in Excel 2024, but it has changed its appearance almost every single time they release a new version of Excel:

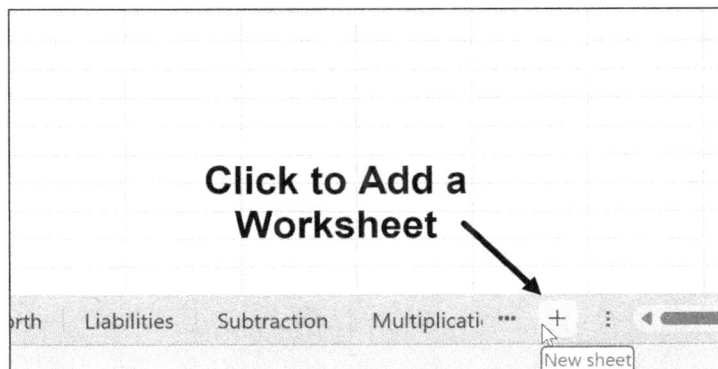

Another option if you can't figure out where that is, is to go to the Cells section of the Home tab, click on the arrow under Insert, and choose Insert Sheet.

Auto-Suggested Text

Auto-suggested text can be very handy to use if you have to enter one of a limited number of choices over and over again and can't easily copy the information from cell to cell.

If you've already typed text into a cell, Excel will suggest that text to you in subsequent cells in the same column.

For example, if in Cell A1, you type STAR, when you go to Cell A2 and type an S, Excel will automatically suggest to you STAR. If you don't want to use the text, then keep typing. If you do, then hit Enter. The suggestion is not case-sensitive, but will use the capitalization of the earlier version when you hit Enter.

There are a few times when auto-suggested text doesn't appear. One is when there are too many empty cells between the one that you already completed, and the one you're now completing. Another is if you have a very long list that you've completed, and the matching entry is hundreds of rows away from the one you're now completing.

Excel will also only make a suggestion if there is a unique match to what you've already typed. So if you have Star 1 and Star 2 in your spreadsheet, and type an S, Excel won't make a suggestion.

It also doesn't make suggestions for numbers, only text or text/number combinations.

Bold Text

Select the cell(s) or text you want bolded and click on the large capital B in the Font section on the Home tab or hold down the Ctrl and B key at the same time. (Ctrl + B)

Center Text

To center the text in a cell or cell(s), select the cells with the contents you want to center, and then go to the Alignment section of the Home tab and click on the lines in the bottom row that are centered:

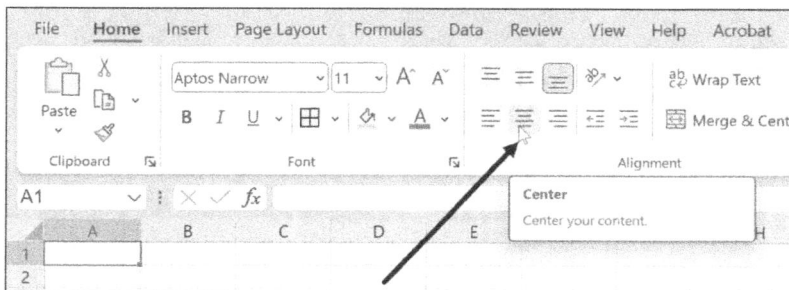

(You can choose from left, center, or right-alignment in that bottom row. The top row lets you choose how text is centered from top to bottom in a cell.)

Column Width

If you need to adjust your column width, you have three options:

1. Right-click on the column and choose Column Width from the dropdown menu. When the box showing you the current column width appears, enter a new column width that is larger or smaller than the current width. (This requires a little too much trial and error for me, but it will always work.)

2. Place your cursor to the right side of the column until it looks like a line with arrows on either side. Left-click and hold while you move the cursor to adjust the column width to what you want it to be.

3. Place your cursor on the right side of the column until it looks like a line with arrows on either side, and then double left-click. This will change the column width to fit the contents of the cells in that column.

You can also select more than one column at once and then use any of the above options to adjust the width of those columns all at once.

Copy the Contents of One Cell To Another

Select the cells that contain the information you want to copy, hold down the Ctrl and C keys at the same time (Ctrl + C) to copy that information, then go to the top left cell of the range where you want to put that information, and hit Enter.

If you want to copy to more than one location, instead of hitting Enter when you click on that cell, hold down the Ctrl and V keys at the same time (Ctrl + V) to paste. You can then click on another cell and use Ctrl + V to paste again. When you're done, use Esc to turn it off.

There are also copy and paste options in the Clipboard section of the Home tab and if you right-click on a cell.

Copy Formatting From One Cell To Another

If you've formatted one cell the way you want it, you can use the format sweeper (that's what I call it because it looks like a broom to me, Microsoft calls it the Format Painter) to apply that format to other cells.

First select the range of cells that have the formatting you want, then click on the little broom in the Clipboard section of the Home tab, and then click in the top left cell in the range of cells where you want to apply that formatting. You may need to select the entire cell range if you're copying formatting from more than one cell.

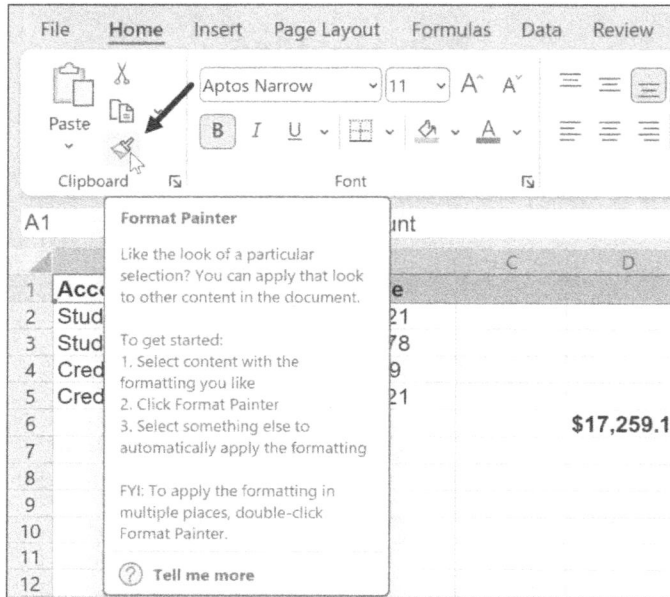

Be careful using the format sweeper because it will change all formatting in your destination cell(s). So, if a cell was already bolded but the one you choose to sweep the formatting from isn't, you'll lose the bold formatting.

(I find this is more of a problem when using the tool in Word than in Excel, but it's still something to watch out for, especially if you have borders around cells.)

Also, the tool will apply formatting to whatever cell you select next, which can be a problem if the cell(s) you want to format aren't right next to the one you try to format sweep from. You need to click on the cell(s) you want formatted. Don't try to use the arrow keys.

It can also be a little tricky if you select multiple cells to sweep the formatting from. It can work, but always check to see if the changes look right after you're done.

If the range of cells you want to sweep from are all identical, just choose one of them and then select the range of cells you want to sweep to.

One more tip: If you double-click the format sweeper you can then apply the formatting to multiple selections. Excel will keep sweeping the format to all the cells you select until you click on the format sweeper again or use Esc to turn it off.

Copy Formulas To Other Cells While Keeping One Value Fixed

We discussed this in the examples, but I want to cover it again. By default when you copy a formula from one location to another, all cell references adjust to the new location. If you have a formula in Cell C1, let's say =A1+B1, and you copy it to Cell C2, the formula will change so that it's now adding Cells A2 and B2. You went down one row so the cell references also adjust by that one row.

If you copy to Cell D1 instead, Excel will change the cell references to B1 and C1 because you moved over a column.

This is one of the biggest strengths of Excel, in my opinion, because it lets you write a formula once and then copy it down thousands of rows.

But sometimes you will want to copy a formula while keeping at least one cell reference fixed. Or part of a cell reference fixed.

To tell Excel not to change that part of a cell reference, use the $ sign in front of the letter or the number for the cell reference.

To keep the column the same, put the $ sign in front of the letter.

$A1

To keep the row the same, put the $ sign in front of the number.

A$1

To keep the reference to a specific cell, put the $ sign in front of both.

$A$1

I love to create what I call two-variable analysis grids. They're very easy to create if you leverage this trick.

Let's say I want to see the various amounts I can earn if I work different hours per week at different pay rates. I can build a grid to look at the possible outcomes for each combination:

	A	B	C	D	E	F	G
1			Pay Rate Per Hour				
2			$8.25	$8.75	$9.25	$9.75	$10.25
3		20	$165.00	$175.00	$185.00	$195.00	$205.00
4		30	$247.50	$262.50	$277.50	$292.50	$307.50
5	Hours Per Week	40	$330.00	$350.00	$370.00	$390.00	$410.00
6		50	$412.50	$437.50	$462.50	$487.50	$512.50
7		60	$495.00	$525.00	$555.00	$585.00	$615.00

The formula I used in Cell C3 is:

=$B3*C$2

By using the $ signs in that formula, that lets me copy and paste that formula to Cells C3 to G7 and still have the formula reference the values in Column B and Row 2 that make up the grid but adjust the formulas otherwise.

In Cell G7 the formula that Excel creates for me is:

$$=\$B7*G\$2$$

which is perfect.

Currency Formatting

If you type a number into a cell in Excel, it'll just show what you type. 25 is 25. $25 is $25.

But sometimes you'll want to just type in 25 and get $25 or $25.00.

To format cells so that the numbers you enter will display as currency, select the cell(s) you want formatted that way, and then go to the Number section of the Home tab, and choose the $ sign. That will apply Accounting format to the cells.

If you prefer the $ sign to be right next to the numbers instead, like I do, use the dropdown menu in the Number section instead. It will say General by default. From there you can choose Currency format. (Or Accounting again.)

Here you can see the dropdown menu with General showing and the $ sign option, as well as what the number 185 looks like with each type of formatting applied:

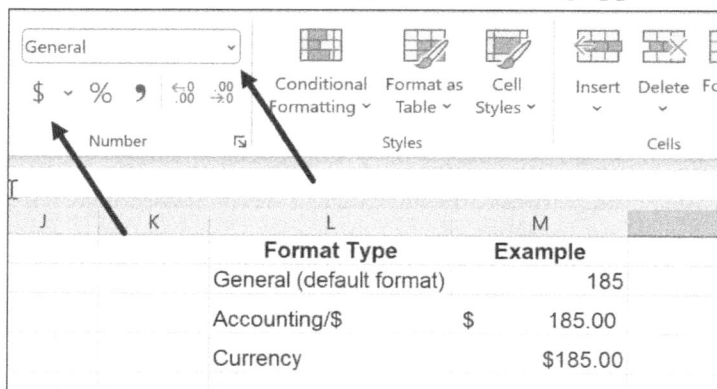

Format Type		Example
General (default format)		185
Accounting/$	$	185.00
Currency		$185.00

You can select cells and then use the zeros with arrows next to them in the Number section of the Home tab to change the number of decimal places that are shown.

For Accounting and Currency format, the default is for two decimal places to show. I sometimes prefer zero.

If you adjust the number of decimal places just remember that behind the scenes Excel still stores that number as-is. So 1.23456 will still be 1.23456 even if you have it display as 1.23.

Date Formatting

Sometimes Excel has a mind of its own about how to format dates. For example, I typed in 1/1 for January 1st, but when I hit Enter Excel showed this as 1-Jan.

It means the same thing, but if I want it to look like 1/1/2025 instead, I have to change the formatting. To do so, select the cell(s) where you want date formatting, go to the Number section on the Home tab, click on the dropdown arrow for format (in this case it says Custom not General), and choose Short Date as the format.

If you want a different format from that one, you can select the cell(s), right-click, and choose Format Cells from the dropdown menu. This will open the Format Cells dialogue box:

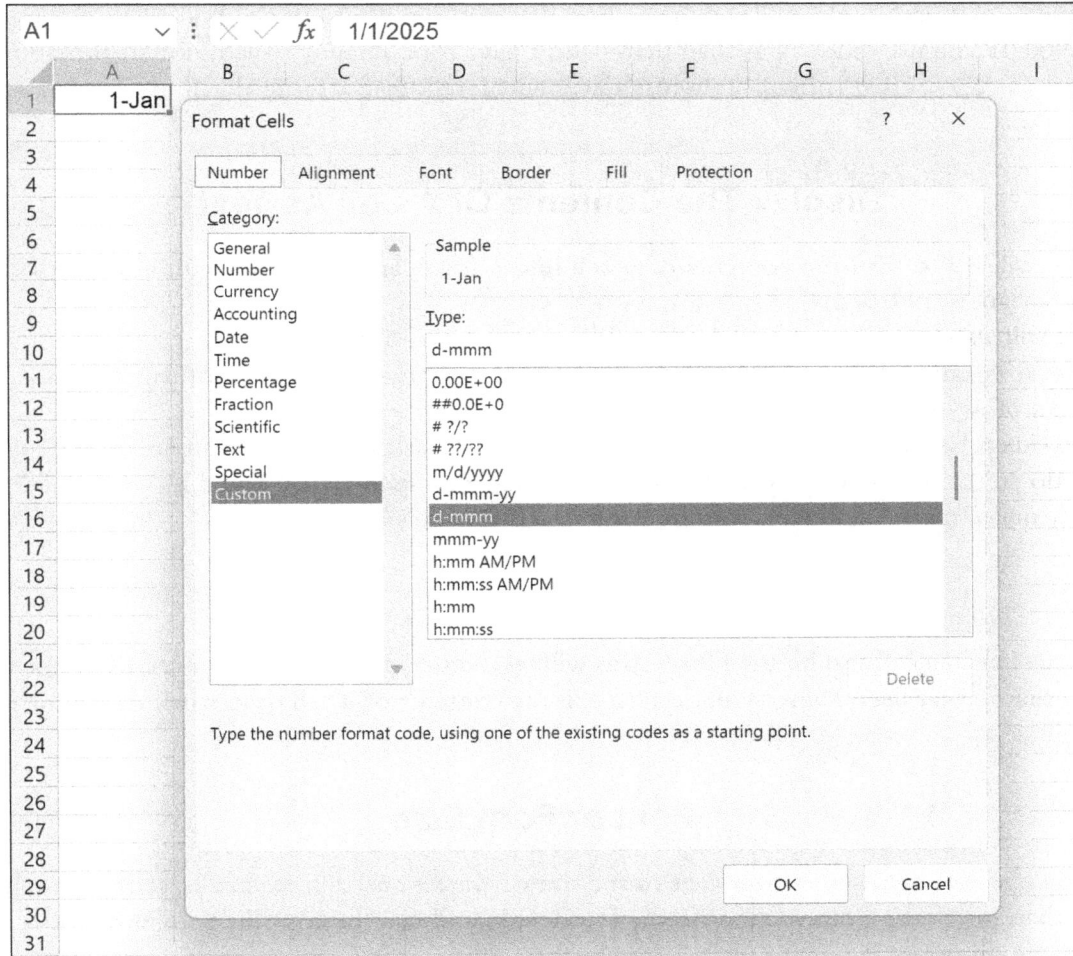

It should open to the Number tab by default, but if it doesn't, click over to the Number tab. Then either choose Date or Custom for the Category on the left-hand side. From there click on the type of date format you want from the list of options under Type.

Excel will show you what the choice you made will look like in the worksheet under Sample.

Excel ALWAYS converts dates to a full date with day of the month, month, and a four-digit year.

If you don't enter that information yourself, Excel will add it. No day of the month, Excel uses the first. No year, Excel uses the current one. A two-digit year, Excel assigns a century based on its internal rules. As of September 2025, for example, 9/15/34 becomes September 15, 1934. So be careful when working with dates that the date is actually what you wanted.

(The reason this happens is because behind the scenes Excel turns dates into numbers. It also means that dates can't go back more than a certain period of time. Type 1 into a cell, format it as a date, and you'll see the earliest date you can use in Excel. For me that's January 1, 1900. If you use older dates than that—and I have for company registration information—Excel can't work with them. I discuss dates and Excel in far more detail in *50 More Excel Functions*.)

Display The Contents Of A Cell As Text

Excel will try to turn the contents of a cell into a formula if you start with a negative sign, equals sign, or plus sign.

It will also sometimes turn text describing a date into a formatted date.

So, for example, December 15, displays as 15-Dec and Excel stores the information as a date instead of as text.

To keep Excel from doing this, type a single quote mark before the contents of the cell. If you do so, Excel will display in the cell everything you typed as you typed it—except for the single quote mark—and will treat the contents of that cell as text.

F2

If you click in a cell and hit the F2 key, this will take you to the end of the contents of the cell. This can be very useful when you need to edit the contents of a cell or to work with a formula in that cell.

Font or Font Size

To change the font used in your cells or the size of the text used in your cells, select the cell(s), and then go to the Font section of the Home tab, and use the font dropdown menu or the font size dropdown menu to make your changes.

Format More Than One Cell At Once

To format more than one cell at once, select all the cells you want formatted, and then apply the formatting you want.

Insert a Cell in a Worksheet

See below for how to insert an entire row or column. Sometimes you just want to insert one cell in the worksheet. In this case, click on where you want to insert the cell, right-click, and select Insert.

You'll be given four choices, Shift Cells Right, Shift Cells Down, Entire Row, Entire Column. (As you can see, the last two choices actually let you insert an entire row or column.)

Shift Cells Right will insert your cell by moving every other cell in that row to the right. Shift Cells Down will insert your cell by moving every other cell in that column down.

Be sure that the option you choose makes sense given the other data you've already entered in the worksheet. Sometimes you'll need to insert more than one cell to keep everything aligned. (To do so, select more than one cell, and then choose to insert.)

Note that inserting cells in a worksheet doesn't change the total number of cells in the worksheet. That is a fixed number. What it's really doing is shifting the information you have in your worksheet to other cells.

Insert a Column or Row

To add an entire row or column, select the row or column where you want your new row or column to go, right-click, and select Insert.

A new row or column should insert automatically, but if it doesn't then choose Entire Row or Entire Column in the dialogue box.

You can also use the Insert dropdown in the Cells section of the Home tab.

Move Across a Row

You can either use the arrow keys (right to move right, left to move left) or the Tab key (Tab to move right, Shift + Tab to move left) to move across a row.

Move the Contents of a Cell or Cells

To move contents of a cell or cells, select the cell(s), and then use Ctrl + X to Cut the contents from where they are. Go to the top left cell of where you want to place those contents, and then use Enter or Ctrl + V to Paste.

You can also right-click on selected cells and use Cut and then Paste or use the Cut and Paste options in the Clipboard section of the Home tab.

With formulas, cutting and moving the cell will keep the formula unchanged. So if your formula was =A2+B2, it will still be =A2+B2. (Whereas with Copy the cell references in the formula will change based upon the number of rows and columns you moved.)

When you move the contents of cells you can only move them to one new location.

Paste Special

Paste just moves content as-is. But there are some special paste options that will take part of the contents of a cell or transform those contents in one way or another.

One I use often is the ability to Paste Special – Values. This lets me paste the results of a formula without keeping the formula that created that result. This can be very useful if I want to "lock in" a result, or if I want to delete the information that a formula was using to return a result.

To do this, copy the cell(s) just the same as you would normally (for me Ctrl + C), and then

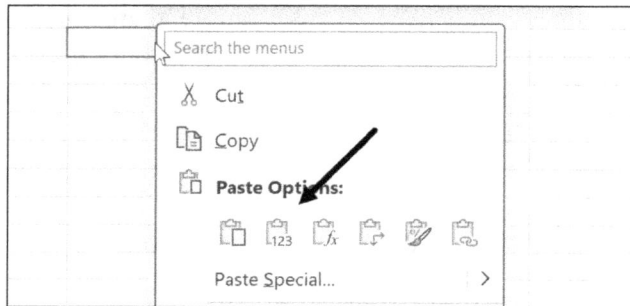

right-click on the cell where you want to paste, and choose from the Paste Options:

Values is the one with numbers in the bottom right corner of the clipboard.

Transpose is another one I sometimes use. It lets you paste numbers that were across a row down a column or down a column across a row. It is the one with two arrows in the corner in Excel 2024. Before I think it was a stack of cells and a row of cells that formed a corner.

Rename A Worksheet

The default names for worksheets in Excel are Sheet1, Sheet2, etc. They're not very useful names if you have information in more than one worksheet.

If you double left-click on a worksheet name (on the tab at the bottom) Excel will highlight the name. You can then type whatever name you want to use and then hit Enter or click away.

There are limits to how long the name can be and what characters you use, but in recent versions Excel will won't let you type a character that isn't allowed or type past the length limit.

Row Height

If you need to adjust your row heights, you have three options:

1. Right-click on the row and choose Row Height from the dropdown menu. When the box showing you the current row height appears, enter a new height that is larger or

smaller than the current value. (This requires a little too much trial and error for me, but it will always work.)

2. Place your cursor below the row number until it looks like a line with arrows pointing up and down. Left-click and hold while you move the cursor to adjust the height to what you want it to be.

3. Place your cursor below the row number until it looks like a line with arrows pointing up and down, and then double left-click. This will change the row height to fit the contents of the cell. For blank rows it will return them to a default height based on your font size for the cells in that row.

You can also select more than one row at once and then use any of the above options to adjust the rows all at once..

Save Backups

If you're trying to create a new worksheet and you're experimenting to get things to work just right, don't be afraid to save multiple copies of the file. Once you have something working, save a copy, work on the next thing, and then save a new copy when you have the next part working.

At the end you can either delete the draft copies or save them for some point down the road when you figure out you messed something up somewhere and need to backtrack.

Just be sure if you do this that you name your files in a way that lets you know which one is the most recent version. For example, I'll call a file ABC File Draft 20250123. And when I save a new version the next day it becomes ABC File Draft 20250124.

I know that the first file is the version I was working on on January 23rd and the second is the draft I was working on on January 24th.

By using that YYYYMMDD format it always sorts in the correct order. I don't recommend using periods in file names even if you can, because it messes with name searches on files.

To save a new version of your file and keep the old one, use File and then choose Save As and give the file an updated name.

If you use Ctrl + S, File ->Save, or the save icon, you will overwrite the earlier version of that file with any edits you made during your current work session.

Select a Row or Column

To select a row or column, click on either the letter of the column or the number of the row.

Undo

Don't be afraid to try things and then undo them if they don't work the way you expected them to. Ctrl + Z is your friend. In most instances, it will undo the last thing you did.

Esc will back you out of what you're currently stuck in.

Sometimes you need Ctrl + Z and then Esc to really clear whatever it was you were trying.

Honestly, the best way to learn Excel is through a little trial and error. Otherwise you'll always be stuck with what someone else showed you. And if you go a little too far and undo something you wanted to keep? Then Redo using Ctrl + Y.

Wrap Text

If there isn't any content in the column next to a cell Excel will automatically display the full contents of the cell by extending into the neighboring columns, but as soon as there is content in the next column, Excel will cut the text off at the edge of the cell.

To make the text in a cell wrap to another line within that same cell, you need to use Wrap Text. Wrap Text takes the text in a cell and displays it on multiple lines, wrapping the text to a new line each time it reaches the edge of the cell.

To use it, select the cell(s) containing the text you want to wrap, go to the Alignment section of the Home Tab, and click on the Wrap Text option.

You can also right-click after you select the cell(s), choose Format Cells from the dropdown menu, go to the Alignment tab of the Format Cells dialogue box, and choose Wrap text under Text Control.

CONTROL SHORTCUTS

Task	Control Shortcut (Ctrl +)
Bold Text	B
Close File	W
Copy	C
Cut	X
Find	F
Italicize Text	I
New File	N
Paste	X
Redo	Y
Save	S
Select Data	Shift + arrow keys A (from within table)
Select All	A
Underline	U
Undo	Z

INDEX

ABOUT THE AUTHOR

M.L. Humphrey is a former stockbroker with a degree in Economics from Stanford and an MBA from Wharton who has spent over twenty-five years as a regulator, consultant, and fraud investigator in the finance industry.

You can reach M.L. at mlhumphreywriter@gmail.com or at mlhumphrey.com.

* * *

To buy ebook titles direct go to https://payhip.com/mlhumphrey.

For Excel templates go to https://payhip.com/mlhumphrey/collection/excel-templates

www.ingramcontent.com/pod-product-compliance
Lightning Source LLC
Chambersburg PA
CBHW081746200326
41597CB00024B/4412